I Believe: Line by Line Through the Creed

Christopher Hayden is curate of Coolfancy and Shillelagh in the parish of Carnew, Ferns Diocese. He holds a PhD in New Testament studies, and has a particular interest in biblical spirituality and the relationship between faith and culture. He has contributed to *Scripture in Church* and is the author of *Lectio Divina* (with John Dutto, 1999), *The Diocesan Priesthood: An Explanation and an Invitation* (2000), *Praying the Scriptures: A Practical Introduction to Lectio Divina* (2001) and *Come, Let Us Adore: Exploring the Crib at Christmas* (2010).

I Believe

Line by Line through

THE CREED

Christopher Hayden

VERITAS

Published 2014 by
Veritas Publications
7–8 Lower Abbey Street
Dublin 1, Ireland
publications@veritas.ie
www.veritas.ie

ISBN 978 1 84730 568 8

10 9 8 7 6 5 4 3 2 1

A catalogue record for this book is available from the British Library.

Designed by Heather Costello, Veritas Publications
Printed by Watermans Printers Ltd, Cork

Veritas books are printed on paper made from the wood pulp of managed forests. For every tree felled, at least one tree is planted, thereby renewing natural resources.

*To the parishioners of Coolfancy and Shillelagh,
with whom I shared these reflections during the
Year of Faith, 2012–13*

Contents

Conclusion

The Creed

I believe in one God,
the Father almighty,
maker of heaven and earth,
of all things visible and invisible.

I believe in one Lord Jesus Christ,
the Only Begotten Son of God,
born of the Father before all ages.
God from God, Light from Light,
true God from true God,
begotten, not made, consubstantial with the Father;
through him all things were made.
For us men and for our salvation
he came down from heaven,
and by the Holy Spirit was incarnate of the Virgin Mary,
and became man.

For our sake he was crucified under Pontius Pilate,
he suffered death and was buried,
and rose again on the third day
in accordance with the Scriptures.
He ascended into heaven
and is seated at the right hand of the Father.

He will come again in glory
to judge the living and the dead
and his kingdom will have no end.

I believe in the Holy Spirit, the Lord, the giver of life,
who proceeds from the Father and the Son,
who with the Father and the Son is adored and glorified,
who has spoken through the prophets.

I believe in one, holy, catholic and apostolic Church.
I confess one Baptism for the forgiveness of sins
and I look forward to the resurrection of the dead
and the life of the world to come. Amen.

Introduction

What is Faith? Approaching the Creed

If someone were to ask you what convictions guide your life, what beliefs you hold and what beliefs hold you, you could begin your answer with the words, 'I believe in one God' and go on to recite the Creed. For a Christian this would, at least in principle, be an excellent and thorough answer to the question, 'What do you believe?' However, if you were to recite the Creed merely as a memorised formula, it might be a very poor answer. It might even be a way of avoiding the question.

The Creed is indeed a rich and meaningful statement of what Christians believe and its very depth invites us to enter in, to explore its meaning, so that what we know by heart is truly an affair of the heart. In these reflections, we will seek to enter in, to explore and to understand. But before we begin to examine what we believe, we will do well to consider what believing is.

To believe is, of course, to have faith, and the Creed is also known as the Profession of Faith. But like a lot of words we hear regularly, the word 'faith' can be so familiar as to be almost empty of meaning. It would be a strange kind of faith that had no effect on the life of the person who held it. It would be a curious believer who said that they accepted all the Church taught, everything the great saints and theologians and prophets and martyrs stood for, but who freely admitted that they didn't believe in letting those convictions interfere in how they lived. That would hardly be an attractive, inviting faith: it would seem eccentric at best, hypocritical at worst.

In contrast, imagine someone who claims to have a great sense of the spiritual, of God, of the 'other side', but who can't tell you a single clear belief they hold. If you ask them to pin down their convictions, they reply that they wouldn't have any truck with anything as limiting as set beliefs. That kind of faith would not be particularly attractive either. It would seem vague, spineless and impractical.

In reality, faith has two fundamental aspects, rather like a coin – a single item with two sides, two inseparable sides. First of all, faith is what we believe. If I say that I have faith, I need to be able to answer the questions, 'Faith in what?' 'What things do you believe?' If the answer to such questions is, 'Well, I don't know, I just believe', then my faith is lacking.

There is a crystal clear content to our faith. It can come as a surprise to many believers that this content is coherent and robust. When we come to understand it, our faith is intellectually solid and satisfying; it adds up, it holds water, it can stand firm in the face of any amount of scepticism and cynicism. Down through history, our Christian faith has held its ground in the face of both external opposition and sinfulness within the Church. The content of our faith has held firm not through luck or accident, but because it is strong, clear, wholesome and wonderful.

But how many of us understand our faith? If someone calls to our door, inviting us to join another religion, and they ask why we are Catholic, can we give an answer? Granted, we aren't all theologians or catechists, but can we at least give an answer to ourselves, in the privacy of our hearts? Or are we left with lingering doubts? A certain number of Catholics are able to say what it is they believe and why, but others are less sure and a large number have very little idea. They believe, perhaps they go to Mass faithfully, but they do not really understand.

Whatever category we might put ourselves in, we may well need to be let in on the great secret that our faith is something strong, clear and intellectually respectable. Christian faith is often questioned, occasionally opposed and sometimes even derided, but when we are well grounded in faith, we find that faith is well able to stand its ground. The truths we believe are a robust treasure, and the Creed is, we might say, the treasure chest.

If one side of the coin of our faith is the content, the things we believe, the other side of the coin is the working out in our lives of what we believe. Faith involves the movement of our hearts and lives, the capacity to turn to God, to trust in him, to offer our lives to him with deep confidence – our hopes, our hardships, our dreams, our disappointments. Yes, we believe certain things, but it is not all 'head stuff' – our hearts are involved too. When people give their lives for their faith – whether it is the ongoing effort to live a decent Christian life, or the decision to follow a radical path of discipleship, or even martyrdom itself – they are not moved by some abstract belief, but by a sense of the reality and the goodness of God. This is the essence of that other side of the coin: a life that trusts in God; a life that – for all its struggles and sins – is turned towards God in hope and trust. If the first side of the coin is what forms the mind, then this second side is what warms the heart. An attentive reading of the Creed can invite us to deepen our trust in God, while clarifying the content of our faith.

In summary, then, faith entails clear, robust beliefs, and a heart that is turned towards God. It is not that we will never experience doubt; and for as long as we live, it will be possible for our hearts to stray. Yet faith remains our anchor and our guide. May this reading of the Creed help us to understand more deeply, and to live what we understand.

I Believe

'I believe.' These words are easy to say, but the actual believing can be a lot more difficult. I believe. But do I *really* believe? Can there be anyone who has not had moments of doubt, who hasn't wondered about this tremendously silent God of ours?

Thankfully, we can say 'I believe' without having to have it all worked out. Those words are for people who want to believe – their use is not limited to those whose belief is rock solid. When we say 'I believe' we are also saying 'I want to believe'. We are saying, just as the father of a troubled child says to Jesus in the gospel, 'Lord, I believe, help my unbelief' (Mk 9:24). This is a lovely prayer, because it tells us that belief can go hand in hand with a genuine struggle to believe.

Moreover, might we not become a bit smug if we had it all worked out? If we never had to struggle, never had a moment's pause, we could run the risk of becoming conceited in our certainty. If I wanted to talk to someone about my doubts, I would far rather approach someone who knew doubt at first-hand. We need not fear our doubts; yes, they can be very real, but the faith we have been given is bigger than doubt. We do not have to wait for perfect belief, before saying 'I believe'.

A standard objection to religious belief is that it is for weak or lazy people who need a ready answer to life's deepest questions. Those who hold this view like to think that unbelief is tougher, more rugged than religious faith. But if we have ever had to wrestle with doubt, we know that this is just not true. Faith calls for real strength and perseverance. Unbelief may pose as the stronger, more independent stance, but it can at times be a refusal to engage with the deepest questions that present themselves to thinking men and women.

What about the many people who are unable to say 'I believe'? People with an intellectual disability, the very young, the very ill? When we say those words, they are not purely private – we can speak them on behalf of others. When an infant is brought for baptism, the parents and godparents say 'I believe' on behalf of the infant. Let us be mindful that when we say 'I believe', we help to carry other people – people who, for whatever reason, are not able to say those words for themselves.

But can we, as believers, really have the nerve to say, 'I've got it right. This belief is correct. Any belief that contradicts it is wrong'? This concern is at the root of another standard objection to religious belief – the notion that it makes people intolerant. But the fact is that we can hold our beliefs with both firmness and gentleness. In practice, the attitude of the vast majority of believers can be summed up as follows: *Yes, I believe certain things, and by the same token, I disbelieve others. But I have no wish to eliminate those who don't share my beliefs. Rather, I want to live out my beliefs in a way that will be a blessing also to those who don't share them.*

But has religious belief not, as a matter of historical fact, caused all sorts of trouble – violence, wars, terrorism?

Wouldn't the world be better off without strong beliefs? There is no doubt that at times, terrible deeds have been masked by a veneer of belief, and evil people have walked beneath a banner of religious faith. The same, however, applies to politics, and the fact that faith and politics can be twisted and warped does not mean that they should both be rejected; rather, what we need is good and wholesome faith – and good and wholesome politics.

Richard Dawkins, one of the most high-profile atheists of recent years, has insisted that religious faith is inherently dangerous, as it constitutes 'an open invitation to extremism'.[1] On the basis of my experience as a priest, I can only observe that the average Sunday morning congregation doesn't exactly look like a threat to humanity! Many of faith's critics overlook the historical fact that considerable intolerance and suppression have been perpetrated by people who believed that religion caused intolerance and suppression. One need think only of the systematic suppression of religious faith during the Soviet era, on the grounds that faith stood in the way of a free and decent life.

But how are we to recognise good, wholesome belief? Happily, the Lord himself has given us a simple criterion: 'By their fruits you shall know them' (Mt 7:16). What we really believe is seen in how we live, in our actions, yet none of us fully lives out our beliefs. There is a lag, a gap, between what we say and how we live. This does not mean that we are roaring hypocrites; it means that we are sinful human beings who also believe in the need for repentance and forgiveness.

---

1. Richard Dawkins, *The God Delusion* (London: Black Swan, 2006), p. 346.

When we say 'I believe', we may imagine that we somehow contain the things we believe, as though our beliefs were in us, inhabiting us. In a much deeper sense, it is the other way around: we inhabit our beliefs. We don't hold them – they hold us. We don't contain the belief that God is real and loving: instead, that belief contains us; it holds and guides us; it deepens and broadens our perspective; it can make a very great difference to our lives.

'I believe. We believe.' Our belief does not sweep away life's burdens, pains and mysteries, but it can see us through. Furthermore, it can help us, in our turn, to see others through.

In One God

'Once you have begun to walk with God, you need only keep on walking with him and all of life becomes one long stroll.'[1] These are not the words of a starry-eyed romantic; they were found in the diary of Etty Hillesum, a young Dutch woman who died in Auschwitz in 1943, having witnessed scenes of appalling cruelty and suffering in the last years of her short life. I quote these words because they make the point that belief in God – in one, good God – has immense potential to transform lives. And not because it is a nice, comforting illusion, but because it captures the truth about reality. The reality of one God is the rock on which believers stand.

Remember that the early Christians were sometimes persecuted – thrown to the lions, burned in front of enthusiastic pagan audiences, hacked to bits by gladiators. When they were being dragged before judges and magistrates, one of the common charges levelled against believers was the charge of atheism. In the Roman Empire at the time, the religion of the state was a religion of many gods, and anyone who rejected the gods was considered to

---

1. Etty Hillesum, *An Interrupted Life: The Diaries and Letters of Etty Hillesum 1941–43* (London: Persephone Books, 1999), pp. 220–1.

be putting the welfare of society at risk. The gods, after all, had to be appeased if they were to continue blessing the empire with political stability and good harvests. But the Christians rejected the gods – they had the gall to insist that there was only one God and that all others were fakes; and so they were accused of atheism. This was, in fact, an entirely logical accusation, and the early Christians' impiety, their disregard of the gods, stirred up hostility and opposition which led, at times, to martyrdom.

Today, we need not fear the kind of persecution which threatened the early Christians, but the insistence that there is only one God runs against a widespread notion of tolerance, which says: 'You believe in your god, I'll believe in mine. You go to your church, I'll go to mine. You have your morality, I'll have mine.' To confine belief to just one God is to be on a collision course with all the other little gods that demand attention and respect. In our politically correct times, it is not considered 'nice' to be exclusive, and to believe in just one God is by definition to exclude belief in others.

It is a feature of human nature that we tend to worship. Our lives, almost independently of any thought-out plan, tend to be directed towards some ultimate centre of meaning and purpose. For some people, power, prestige, pleasure or security come to be virtually objects of worship. For Christians, the only final goal is God, the one and only God. At any given time, there may be lesser gods within us and about us, clamouring for attention; little gods of resentment, ambition, lust, greed, despair. But our faith helps us to remain focused on the one, true God, so that we are less prone to being led astray by those lesser gods, or swamped by unavoidable human concerns.

Seeking to direct our lives towards God is not simply a matter of piety or devotion. To have God – the one God – as our final reference point is tremendously freeing. Consider those who are in a state of despair, or deep anxiety; those who are tormented by financial worries, or worries about their health or their loved ones. If these burdens are the ultimate reality, if there is nothing or no-One beyond them, then what is the reason for hope? Faith can give hope, and far from insulating us from life's concerns or from the sufferings of loved ones, this hope equips us to bear burdens and face challenges.

The lasting foundation for hope is belief in one God, in a God who is greater than any desire, fear or suffering. If everything were to crumble, we would be blessed to be able to say, with the psalmist, 'The Lord is my rock' (Ps 18:2). This is a conviction that we should allow ourselves to rest in, to draw great comfort from. Happily, we do not have to be people of enormous faith or holiness to have a deep belief in the One God as our foundation.

A well-known prayer of St Teresa of Ávila captures this attitude of fundamental hope and trust:

Let nothing trouble you/Let nothing frighten you.
Everything passes/God never changes.
Patience/Obtains all
Whoever has God/Wants for nothing.
God alone is enough.[2]

---

2. *Catechism of the Catholic Church* (Dublin: Veritas–Libreria Editrice Vaticana, 1994), 227.

The Father

Names are important. Those of us who have trouble remembering names know what it is like to hope for patience and understanding from people whose names we feel we really should know. If you have ever forgotten someone's name, then apologetically asked them to tell you again, only to forget it once more, you will know that names are not just labels of convenience: they are part of us; they are part of how we, as persons, are recognised.

God has a name, a name by which he is recognised. In the Bible, there are various ways of naming and referring to God, but it was Jesus who finally told us how to address him: God is 'Father'. When his disciples asked him to teach them to pray, Jesus said to them, 'When you pray, say: "Our Father …"' We can say that 'Father' is God's 'Christian name', because it is the name given to him by Christ.

What do fathers do? First of all, fathers know their children. A father names, recognises, calls, corrects and provides for his children. A father suffers when his children suffer, when they go astray, when they are ill or in danger. A father rejoices when his children rejoice.

We know, of course, that human fathers, like everyone else, have their limitations. They can be less than they should be – sometimes, sadly, a great deal less. A wise person once remarked that one of the tasks we need to negotiate in order to become mature human beings is to forgive our parents for not being perfect. We might add that we also need to forgive ourselves for ever having expected another human being to be perfect.

Every earthly father is less than perfect, and some people carry heavy burdens of sadness and pain on account of the shortcomings of their fathers. For those who have had particularly mixed or negative experiences of fatherhood, it may come as really good news that God is not *a* Father – God is *the* Father. We do not judge God by the yardstick of human fatherhood; instead, we can bring to God the Father any brokenness and suffering that arise from the experience of human fatherhood. As for the blessings that arise from human fatherhood, the love and care and selflessness that most fathers show most of the time – these can be signposts towards the fatherhood of God.

Jesus went a step further than simply telling us to call God 'Father'. He himself addressed God as 'Abba' (Mk 14:36). That word is from Jesus' mother tongue, Aramaic. It is the word small children used when addressing their father; it is the word for 'Daddy'. We need not bother asking little children why they call their father 'Daddy'. The whole point is that it is not something that has to be thought about: it is a spontaneous expression of affection and trust. It is something a child just does.

So when St Paul encourages us to cry out 'Abba, Father …' (Rm 8:15), he is inviting us to be spontaneous, to trust. He is inviting us to step away, at least for a moment, from all the doubts, all the analysis, all those very grown-up questions that begin with the words 'why should I?' The fact is that we never can reason our way to a loving Father; we do not invent love and nurturing – these things invent us, they (or their absence) make us who we are.

If we wait for all the answers before trusting, we have decided not to trust. If we wait for certainty before taking a step, we have decided to stand still. But faith says to us: 'Trust, trust in the reality of a loving Father-God, and take things from there.'

The words with which the Creed begins, 'I believe in one God, the Father ...' are very powerful words. They are like a foundation on which we stand, and on which we build. They can speak to the deepest part of us, to the child inside each one of us – a child made for love and goodness; a child who can be hurt and disappointed by the absence of love and goodness. There is a deep and flawless alignment between the words 'I believe in one God, the Father ...' and our human nature. Those words do no violence to us; although they are the words of a trusting child, they do not infantilise us. Quite the contrary: they encourage us to live a life of trust instead of fear; a life that is focused outwards rather than turned in on itself.

'I believe in God, the Father.' This is the language of trust, rather than a phrase that demands to be analysed to death. As we hear these words and learn them afresh, let us allow them to build us up, so that we can build our lives on them.

Almighty

God the Father is all-powerful, almighty. This is a fundamental Christian belief, and it is a belief that often has a question hot on its heels: 'If God is all-powerful, almighty, then why doesn't he do something about suffering and tragedy in the world? Why does he not intervene a bit more?'

It would be very hard to find any thoughtful believer who has not asked what God is up to, why he permits certain things to happen, why he does not intervene to save people in distress. It is virtually impossible not to ask questions like these at times. We could truthfully say that these questions are part and parcel of mature faith: at the very least, they show that we are trying to take our faith seriously, rather than coasting along with a set of comfortable platitudes.

Such questions are far from being theoretical abstractions. For people in situations of suffering or distress, they can seem closer to a matter of life and death. Religious questions that begin with the word 'why' are very often good and necessary questions. One of the most dramatic books in the entire Bible is all about a man's attempt to take God to task over the issue of innocent suffering: the Book of Job shakes a fist at heaven and looks for answers.

The world can be cruel and unpredictable, and it can seem hard to square suffering and evil with a God who is both loving and all-powerful. Faith does not eliminate suffering, nor does it offer a satisfactory reason for each experience of pain. What our faith offers is not so much reasons as resources: it equips us to keep going, with dignity and hope. Indeed, many people who come through great suffering arrive at the conviction that God's power works not so much by the elimination of suffering, as in and through suffering.

There is no simple answer: trying to square an almighty, loving God with the presence of terrible suffering, innocent suffering, can be like trying to square a circle. Yet common sense tells us that to abandon belief in God does not make suffering one bit more tolerable, nor does unbelief provide any extra answers. The sad fact is that when people abandon faith on account of suffering, they can be abandoning the very possibility that their suffering may have a deeper meaning.

Here we are drawn – if we allow ourselves to be drawn – into another question: the question of why so many suffering people throughout history have found comfort and strength in their faith – faith in a silent and apparently inactive God. While faith in an almighty Father does not deal in platitudes or pat answers, it clearly has a long and worthy track record in helping those who suffer.

We must, however, be bluntly realistic: for those who are in the throes of suffering, those who look on helplessly as loved ones suffer, no discussion avails. Indeed, any discussion could sound like an attempt to get God off the hook. But this is where we come to the heart of the Christian approach to suffering. Far from 'getting God off the hook', our Christian faith recognises that God willingly put himself on the hook of human suffering. On the cross,

Christ took on himself the very deepest torment, despair and abandonment, to the point of crying out, 'My God, my God, why have you abandoned me?' These words remind us that for Christians, the 'mystery of suffering' is also the mystery of Christ's participation in suffering.

Faith in a crucified Lord does not brush away questions about suffering and an almighty God, but it insists – it promises – that just as happened on the cross, suffering and death do not have the last word. The question 'why?' is not the only question that suffering poses. This question looks backwards, to the source of suffering: how it came to be, why it was permitted. But there are also forward-looking questions that suffering can lead us to ask; questions such as: 'Where to from here?' 'Now that this has happened, what can I do?' Our faith may not give satisfactory answers to the backward-looking questions, but it gives us a clear answer to these forward-looking questions: it urges us to help bear people's burdens, and to bear our own with trust.

'Where was the almighty God when this terrible thing happened? Where is he, now that I have this burden to bear?' Let's be clear: these are fair questions, reasonable questions, questions that thinking people can hardly avoid. But they are not the only questions, nor are they necessarily always the best questions. Let us never forget the question that goes like this: 'How does my faith in God the Father *almighty* invite me to bear whatever burdens life brings to me, and how can that same faith help me to help others?' God our almighty Father does not erect an impenetrable wall between his children and suffering. Instead, his power breaks through the impenetrable wall that suffering can sometimes erect.

Maker of Heaven and Earth, of All Things Visible and Invisible

The opening words of the Bible are 'In the beginning, God made the heavens and the earth.' This means that when the Creed uses the expression 'maker of heaven and earth', it takes us right back to the foundations of reality.

Neither the Creed nor the Bible set out to give us scientific details regarding the manner in which God created, and we need not get bogged down in details of modern science or of the theory of evolution. We do not have to reconcile details from the book of Genesis with the details of science or geology, and believers are perfectly free to accept any scientific theories about how the universe came to be. Science and theology are two different languages, but there is only one truth, and both of these languages try to understand and describe the aspects of the truth that concern them.

The Bible and the Creed insist that God created; science insists on the reality of evolution. There need not be any contradiction here, and one of the Church's catechisms very sensibly observes that 'evolution presupposes the existence of something that can develop'.[1] If the world has evolved, if the human race has come about through evolution, then we can thank God for his evolutionary handiwork.

When the Creed says that God the Father created, it is saying something truly marvellous. Modern physics tells us that there are just four fundamental energies in the universe: gravity, electromagnetic force, strong nuclear force and weak nuclear force. The Creed, for its part, tells us that the fundamental energy of the universe is fatherhood: 'God, the Father, created ...'

There is no contradiction here. If God the Father can weave this wonderful universe from just four forces, then praised be he! Beneath the wonderful complexity of the universe, our faith insists that creation has been *fathered* into existence. We are not cosmic flukes or random collections of particles. We have not come about by chance: we have been fathered, called, loved into existence. We have come from the mind and heart of God. This is our origin and with it we have also been given a destiny: life with God, a life which is the fullness of the life and beauty that this world offers.

No, we are not here by chance; yes, we have been fathered. We owe our origin to God, and the same is true of our ongoing, continued existence: we exist from God. Saint Edith Stein, a convert from the Jewish faith, a Carmelite nun, and one of the twentieth century's most influential philosophers, wrote: 'In the knowledge that being holds me, I rest secure.'[2]

God is the source of all being – nothing that happens, nothing that is, is hidden from him. The conviction that

---

1. *YouCat* (San Francisco: Ignatius Press, 2011), p. 42.
2. Edith Stein, *Essential Writings* (Modern Spiritual Masters Series) (New York: Orbis, 2008), p. 68.

God, the maker of all things, is in charge is a life-altering conviction. It sustained St Edith Stein as she went to her death in the concentration camp at Auschwitz. The saint insisted that the conviction that we are in the loving care of our creator-God is an intelligent, rational conviction – as rational as the trust a small child has in its mother or father: 'if a child were living in the constant fear that its mother might let it fall, we should hardly call this a rational attitude.'[3] We are not our own creators; we have our being from God and in God. There will always be questions and there will often be doubts, but it is eminently rational and sane to place our trust in God our creator.

The Creed tells a story. It begins by telling us that God created all things, and it ends by looking forward to 'the life of the world to come'. That is our story: we have been *fathered*, called into being by God, and we are destined for eternal life. None of us remembers our coming into being, and we do not know what the life after this one is like. So here we are, between two mysteries, between our beginning and our end. We are somewhere in the middle of the story, muddling along. Sometimes it is indeed a muddled middle.[4] But the story which the Creed outlines for us isn't just going somewhere: it is taking us with it. We are caught up in God's plan for his creation, and our faith in God, our Father and Creator, helps us to make sense of this muddled middle.

Finally, the Creed tells us that God has created 'all things visible and invisible'. We do well to bear in mind that there is much more to reality than meets the eye. There

---

3. Ibid.
4. Cf. R. Paul Stevens and Michael Green, *Living the Story: Biblical Spirituality for Everyday Christians* (Grand Rapids: Eerdmans, 2003), p. ix.

is a spiritual world; there are spiritual powers, both good and evil. As St Paul reminds us, it is not merely against human enemies that we have to struggle, but 'against the sovereignties and powers who originate the darkness of this world, the spiritual army of evil' (Eph 6:12). Dramatic language, perhaps, but it holds no terrors for those who are caught up in the drama of a life lived with God, our Father and our Creator.

I Believe in One Lord Jesus Christ

What is the heart of the Christian faith? What is it essentially about? The heart of the matter is not a teaching or a moral outlook, but a person: the person of Jesus Christ. There is no teaching or doctrine or practice that can be sifted out, distilled or detached from the person of Christ, so that we might say, 'Here it is, this is what it's about.' The essence of our faith is, to repeat, the person of Christ. One of the great theologians of the twentieth century puts it very simply: 'Christian belief ... stands or falls with the historical person of Jesus. Christian belief is Jesus!'[1]

It is strange, then, and more than a little sad, that so many Christians have a very strong sense that their faith involves teachings, rules and practices, but have little or no sense of the person of Christ. They have received the rules, the practices, the morality, but have never encountered the person to whom all these things are a response.

It is worth repeating, the heart of our faith is Christ: 'I believe in one Lord Jesus Christ.' If we were to leave out the

---

1. *Romano Guardini: Spiritual Writings* (Modern Spiritual Masters Series) (New York: Orbis, 2005), p. 116.

person of Christ, we would be a bit like a man for whom being married meant working to maintain a household, ferrying children about and putting out the bins, but who had no personal relationship with his wife! The other things may, of course, be part and parcel of a marriage, but without the relationship, the heart is missing. Likewise, a faith that consists in doing all the necessary things, but that doesn't involve a relationship with Christ as Lord, is a faith that is impoverished. We are being offered more than we realise.

There is a lot of silliness spoken, written and broadcast about Jesus. If the 'silly season' in the political world is during the summer, when journalists are desperate for news, the silly season for Christian faith is around Christmas and Easter, when there is nearly always someone poised to tell us that we have had it wrong all along. Here, once again, those words that we say four times in the Creed, the words 'I believe', are hugely important. Our faith is not built on some hazy notions, but on a clear foundation. When we insist, for example, that Jesus is Lord, that he is God's Son, we are being no more unreasonable or dogmatic than an engineer who says 'I believe in gravity'. For a Christian, the idea that belief in Christ is something that was imposed by the early Church as a way of exercising control is about as sensible as the notion that belief in gravity limits human freedom.

Once, in the run-up to Christmas, I heard a novelist being interviewed on the radio. During the course of the interview, he tossed out as a historical fact the notion that the content of belief was not considered important for the first several centuries of Christianity, and that the only thing that mattered was that believers 'entered into the story'

– whatever that might mean. He was not contradicted or corrected; it is a free country, and he was left free to dismiss belief in the person and Lordship of Christ as the invention of a cynical, power-crazed group of men. We need not dwell on this, but it is important for us to realise that the beliefs at the heart of our faith are often – even routinely – misrepresented, misunderstood or greeted with scepticism.

When we say 'I believe in one Lord Jesus Christ', we are asserting an important human and political right. We are insisting that as Lord, Christ is our ultimate authority. At a time when many of us have become somewhat cynical and jaded about politics, it may warm our hearts to recall that when we affirm the lordship of Jesus Christ, we are saying that no state, no politician, no leader, no law will overturn or overrule the judgment of an informed Christian conscience. We do not say, in the Creed, 'I believe that Christ is a Lord'. Rather, we insist that he is *the* Lord, the *only* Lord; the authority above all authorities. This is an important human freedom to assert, at a time in history when the reach of the state appears to grow ever longer. Indeed, the state may reach far into our lives, but it cannot reach into that personal space in which we affirm that Christ, and nothing or no one else, is our final authority. This is why, from the very beginning of Christianity, people got in trouble over the belief that Christ is the one and only Lord. What about Herod? What about Caesar? Those people got angry, and it did not end there: in Nazi Germany, a priest was imprisoned for daring to call Christ not the *Lord* but simply the *leader*. That was Hitler's title: *Der Führer*; his supporters were not happy about it being used for anyone else.

All of this means that when we say the words 'I believe in one Lord Jesus Christ', we are saying something that is at one and the same time both profoundly personal and profoundly political. On a personal level, we affirm that Jesus is our Lord – a real, living person, to whom we look, to whom we pray. The insistence that Jesus, and only Jesus, is our final authority can have the profoundest of political consequences. Our faith in Christ, therefore, ranges from the personal to the political, and covers everything in between. Let us treasure it!

The Only Begotten Son of God

The Creed is a carefully compiled list of statements, a list that draws together the core truths of our Christian faith, so that when we recite it, we are, so to speak, setting out our stall, stating where we stand.

When we want to emphasise something, to make our point without leaving any room for doubt, we often repeat ourselves. This is just what the Creed does when it comes to the insistence that Jesus is divine, that he is truly God. The Creed does not simply state that Jesus is the Son of God, and then move on to the next truth. Instead, the Creed lingers over this truth, spelling it out repeatedly by means of a kind of studied, solemn repetition, which includes no less than seven different expressions. Jesus, 'the only begotten Son of God,' is also:

Born of the Father before all ages
God from God
Light from Light
True God from true God
Begotten, not made
Consubstantial with the Father

Each of those phrases tells its own truth, yet there is a strong element of repetition. The Creed wants to leave us in no doubt whatsoever: Jesus is divine; Jesus is God. What is a Christian? A Christian is a person who believes that Jesus is God, and who lives out of that belief. Yes, Jesus was born a baby, and grew up to be a man – the Creed will also remind us of that. But Jesus is more than just a man; more, even, than an outstandingly good man. One of the biggest debates in the early Church was over the nature of Jesus. Some people insisted that he was divine, but downplayed or denied his humanity; others insisted that he was human, but downplayed or denied his divinity. At a certain point, the teaching Church intervened and said, 'Enough! Jesus is fully God and fully man.'

Lest this sound a bit abstract, let us pause and ask how it is relevant to us. Here is an image that captures something of how utterly relevant it is to us that Jesus is both God and man. If you are trying to cross a deep chasm, or a canyon, you need something that is firmly connected to both sides – a rope, a cable, a bridge. But whatever kind of structure it might be, it is of no heavenly or earthly use unless it is firmly anchored on both sides of the chasm.

Jesus is firmly anchored in God; and he is firmly anchored in humanity. And so it is in Jesus, and only in him, that we can cross the chasm between the frailty and weakness of our human nature, and the infinite strength and goodness of God. At the end of our lives, it is in Jesus that we cross the impossible chasm between death and life. When I pray to Jesus, I am not praying to someone who is simply a good and inspiring human being: I am praying to the one who can reach me in my humanity, to the one who can find me where I am, and who can raise me up – ultimately beyond death.

We might ask ourselves: what 'impossible chasms' have I experienced, or might I yet experience? To whom have I turned, or to whom will I turn? Our faith invites us to turn to Jesus. As man, he knows all about pain and betrayal and misunderstanding and fear. As God, he knows how to deal with them. For us believers, it is no trifling matter that the man Jesus is the Son of God.

Someone once said that if Jesus were only heavenly, he would be no earthly use to us, and if he were only earthly, he would be no heavenly use. He is both heavenly and earthly. We know from the historical record that the man Jesus existed, preached, gathered followers, and was crucified. This information is found not only in the Bible, but also in ancient Roman historical sources. The Creed wants to ensure that the clarity of those historical facts is accompanied by clarity regarding the divinity of Jesus, and that is why it is insistent to the point of repetition.

A final thought: Jesus, the only begotten Son of God, shared our humanity so that we might be sons and daughters of God. Jesus is God's Son by nature; we are called to be God's children by *adoption*. Saint Paul tells us that we have received 'a spirit of adoption' (Rm 8:15). As adopted children, we are beloved of the Father, precious to him. This short poem, written by a woman for her beloved adopted child, conveys something of the reality of God's love for his adopted children:

Not flesh of my flesh,
Nor bone of my bone,
but still miraculously my own.

Never forget for a single minute;
You didn't grow under my heart
but in it.[1]

As Christians, we are called to trust that we have a space
in God's heart, along with his only begotten Son, who is our
Lord and our brother.

---

1. Quoted in Paul Murray OP, *Doors to the Sacred: A Meditation on the Hail Mary* (London: DLT, 2010), p. 57. Murray states that the poem is most often attributed to Fleur Heyliger.

Born of the Father
Before All Ages.
God from God, Light
from Light, True God
from True God

As we make our way through the Creed, we will do well to remind ourselves that the Creed was not composed as proof – it was not written to prove that God exists, or that Jesus is his Son. When we recite the Creed, we are giving expression to the faith that we already hold. But sometimes the very act of repeating our beliefs helps us to grow in them; just as the words 'I love you' do more than simply communicate information about how the person speaking them happens to feel. Those three little words don't simply express love: they actually strengthen it. Likewise, reaffirming and repeating the truths of our faith can strengthen our faith.

When we recite the Creed, we say that Jesus was 'born'. This is something we all have in common with him: our arrival in this world as tiny, needy, vulnerable human beings. But of course, the Creed immediately adds that Jesus was born 'of the Father before all ages'. This is something we do not have in common with him. We came into existence when we were conceived, and it is virtually impossible for us to get our minds around the fact that there was a time when we did not exist. Jesus' human nature came into existence when he was conceived, but as God's Son, he existed from eternity, before time; there was never a time when he did not exist. It would sound extremely odd if we were to say, 'I took on human nature when I was conceived.' Before our conception, there simply was no 'I'. We did not exist. The Son of God did. He already had an existence, but he agreed to share fully in ours; he was utterly rich, and he agreed to share in our poverty; utterly self-sufficient, and he agreed to share in our weakness and vulnerability. That is the kind of Lord we believe in, the Lord who was 'born of the Father before all ages', and yet was born one of us.

I once read a book review in which the reviewer described a large volume of theology as 'both exhaustive and exhausting'. In these reflections on the Creed, I am not attempting to be exhaustive (and hopefully I will not be too exhausting either!). In the phrases 'God from God,/ Light from Light,/ true God from true God', the only word I want to highlight is the word 'Light'. Yes, Jesus is God from God, true God from true God; but one identifying characteristic the Creed singles out is *light*.

Jesus is light. In the gospel he tells us: 'I am the light of the world' (Jn 8:12). Then he adds: 'Those who follow me will not walk in darkness but will have the light of life.' Our ordinary way of speaking links light and truth: to know the truth is to be enlightened. Not to know something is to be in the dark about it. The early Christians used to call themselves the 'enlightened'. Still today, during the baptismal ceremony, when the child's baptismal candle is lit, the priest says to the child's parents: 'Receive the light of Christ.'

A question we might do well to reflect on is: 'In what way does my faith enlighten me? What clarity does it bring me that I would not otherwise have?' If we are uncertain, then the good news is that the best is still ahead of us. Faith in Christ, to be sure, does not offer a ready answer to every question life puts to us. But it can help us to see the questions themselves in a different light.

Here is just one example of how faith can enlighten us – of how it enlightens countless believers. There is a great and fundamental difference between how our secular culture sees suffering and how believers see it. Our secular culture tends to see faith in the light of suffering. Believers see suffering in the light of faith. The secular mind thinks: 'Look at all the suffering in the world; faith must be nonsense.' The believer, in contrast, because he or she has faith, rejects the idea that suffering is nonsense, that it is meaningless. From the point of view of unbelief, suffering casts darkness on faith; from the point of view of belief, faith casts light on suffering. This is not 'whistling in the dark', as unbelievers and sceptics would like us to believe. There is a world of difference between whistling in the dark and looking towards the light.

I will finish with a brief reflection that you might call to mind when you are visiting a church with stained-glass windows. How does stained glass work? It is stained glass whether we look at it from outside or inside the church. But it is entirely different, depending on which of those views we are taking. From outside, stained glass is dark and dull; it could even seem like a waste of what should be a clear, bright window. But from inside, it is a different matter entirely. From inside, we see the colour, the form and the beauty of the stained glass.

Sceptics may lament the dullness they see from the outside. We are invited to take a different view: to come inside, to inhabit our faith in Christ, and in this way to see the beauty of our faith and the light and hope Christ offers.

Begotten, Not Made, Consubstantial with the Father

This is the second mention in the Creed of the fact that Jesus is 'begotten'. We have already heard that he is 'the only begotten Son of God.' But before we try to unwrap the meaning contained in those words, let us stand back for a moment and ask: Why all the words? Why all the nit-picking precision? Is this not just irrelevant hair-splitting? After all, when we come to Mass, or when we pray, we are neither thinking *of* nor thinking *in* this rather dry terminology. If I visit someone who is ill, and I want to pray with them or keep them company in their struggle, they will not find it particularly useful or uplifting if I say to them, 'By the way, as you lie on your sick bed, keep in mind the fact that Jesus is "begotten, not made, consubstantial with the Father".'

The solemn language of the Creed is like the foundation of a house – it is absolutely essential. However, we do not enter the house through the foundation: we go in through the door. The 'door' of our everyday faith is the language and attitude of trust in God. Those words of the Creed, 'begotten, not made, consubstantial with the Father', are not the everyday language of prayer and belief and struggle and doubt. But this does *not* mean that those words are irrelevant. When we walk over a picturesque bridge, we will probably be more interested in enjoying the view than in pondering the engineering aspects of the structure that is keeping us from falling into the river. But that does not mean that the engineer's textbooks and formulas are irrelevant.

Granted, the Blessed Trinity is not an engineering problem! When many great minds and saints set themselves to understand God, they were not trying to solve a problem or come up with a formula. What they sought to do was safeguard a mystery. God will always be infinitely bigger than human intelligence, and the Creed does not set out to *explain* the Trinity. In effect, the saints and scholars who gave us the Creed were saying, 'If you keep within these lines and limits, then you won't go astray; if you accept these fundamental truths, then no, you won't understand God, but yes, you will avoid the risk of fundamentally misunderstanding God.'

This means that when we recite the Creed, we are acknowledging that our faith is rooted in the prayer and reflection of the saints and scholars and pastors who gave us the Creed. We do not invent our belief – we receive it as a gift. Happily, we do not have to plumb the theological depths every time we recite the Creed. Whenever we recite this statement of our belief, we are saying that our faith has deep, strong roots; it is well founded; it is a gift from God that has been received and lived, and whose power and goodness is well established.

Back to those words, 'begotten, not made'. From a human perspective, to be begotten means to be brought to life, to be brought into existence, and so there seems to be the makings of a contradiction in those words. If Jesus is begotten, then surely he is made? Here, the Creed is telling us something else about the relationship between Jesus and the Father: this is a relationship of begetting, in which Jesus receives himself from the Father.

Think of a person who is in love. People in love know that in a very real sense they are receiving themselves from the person they love; they feel that they have never been more alive, more real, more truly themselves; they are given life, 'begotten' by the one they love. This is the way it is with God, but always, permanently, eternally. The Son receives his whole self from the Father, he is begotten of the Father. But things were never any other way – there was no beginning, no initial moment where the Son came into being. And so, the Creed says that the Son is 'begotten, not made'.

If that sounds a little abstract, then let us remember that our faith is founded on the conviction of a permanent, unchanging love. There is nothing at all abstract about the *absence* of permanence in love. When the love between people ends, as it occasionally does, the consequences can be very concrete indeed. The fact that our faith is founded on permanent love is immensely practical: it is as practical as magnetic north. We cannot see it, yet we can safely navigate by it.

Jesus is also 'consubstantial with the Father'. Among the early Christians were some who argued about the nature of Jesus. Is he God, or is he man? Some said one, some said the other. Some said a bit of one and more of the other. But the most careful reflection on biblical truth has insisted that Jesus is *both* God *and* man; *fully* God and *fully* man. Those words, 'consubstantial with the Father', capture the fact that Jesus, although fully human, is indeed God. He has two natures – human and divine – but only one self, one person, one substance, which he shares with the Father.

After the resurrection, when Jesus appeared on the shore of Lake Galilee, the disciple John saw him from the boat and said, 'It is the Lord.' The Creed puts great and repeated stress on the divinity of Jesus, and this is so that we can repeat with John the disciple: 'It is the Lord.'

This Lord of ours is no abstraction. Let me finish with some lovely words of encouragement from one of the great saints of the ancient Church, St Ambrose of Milan:

> In Christ we have everything …
> If you want to heal your wound, he is the doctor.
> If you are burning with fever, he is the fountain.
> If you are in need of help, he is strength.
> If you are in dread of death, he is life.
> If you are fleeing the darkness, he is light.
> If you are hungry, he is food.

Through Him All Things Were Made

This is the second time the Creed mentions creation. We have already heard that God, the Father almighty, is the 'maker of heaven and earth'. Now, we are being told that it was *through* the Second Person of the Trinity, the 'one Lord, Jesus Christ', that all created reality came into being. Our Christian faith makes it very clear that creation was not a fluke or a mistake, but was willed and planned by God – the Father and Son, working together. The third person of the Trinity, the Holy Spirit, is also part of this co-operative venture, and the Creed teaches us about the Spirit's role after its teaching on the Son.

Creation, to repeat, is not a mistake or a fluke. The Creed tells us not once but twice that God wanted creation, planned it, desired it. At the time of Christ, and in the earliest days of Christianity, many pagan religions taught their followers that creation was evil and that salvation meant escaping from all material things, including the body. But the Christians, just like the Jews, our older brothers and sisters in the faith, insisted that created reality is good, a blessing, a manifestation of God's wisdom and care.

There have been times when Christians fell into mistaken or warped views, forgetting that all creation is good. At certain times, for example, there has been a great mistrust of human sexuality, to the point where it has been seen more as a threat to salvation than as a gift of God. Human sinfulness and weakness can certainly make this a vulnerable gift, but the Church has never taught that human sexuality is anything other than a gift from God, for which men and women should be grateful, and which should be carefully guarded against the excesses and blindness to which our sinfulness can give rise.

'[T]hrough him all things were made.' Imagine how our way of walking on this earth might be changed for the better if we took those words to heart: 'Through him, through Jesus, the Son of God, all things were made.' Some years back, it was fashionable to speak of the 'greening' of the Church, a term which could suggest that believers were finally catching up with the environmental movement. But the Creed has been green all along! Our faith invites us to value God's creation, given to us as a gift.

In his Letter to the Romans, St Paul writes that God has been recognisable, since the beginning of the world, in the things he has made (cf. Rm 1:20). Yet we do not always see the goodness and loveliness in the world. Why is it that we can be blind to goodness? Sometimes there are obvious reasons: people who are ill, or grieving, or anxious can have their energies and attention consumed. Yet there is a forgetfulness that affects practically everyone to some extent: we routinely forget that reality itself is a gift.

Imagine yourself in your favourite shop, with a reasonably generous, but not unlimited, voucher. How will you look at the things in that shop? You won't be there to admire; you'll be there to get! You'll be calculating, working out: 'How much can I get? What's the best way to use my voucher? What's the best value?' Now, instead of the shop, put yourself in front of your favourite view, or listening to your favourite piece of music or reading a favourite poem. In this case, there is no need for calculation; all you have to do is open your eyes, your mind, your soul, and it is yours to enjoy. We are broken and limited creatures, and we have a great desire for security. Our insecurity can lead us to look at reality as though it were a shop in which to get things, rather than as something lovely, something simply *there*, a gift and a blessing. Those words from the Creed can speak to this brokenness and insecurity of ours: 'through him all things were made'. We have to shop, to get, to make ends meet, and there can be real struggle involved. The faith which we profess in the Creed does not urge us to be naïve about reality; rather, it reminds us that Christ is the heart of reality.

Some people imagine that it is naïve and unrealistic to thank and praise God even in the midst of difficulties. Our faith would insist that it is naïve and unrealistic to imagine that we can navigate life's difficulties if we never take a moment to thank and praise God. '[T]hrough him all things were made.' Let us, then, give praise and thanks to Christ, for his goodness in creation and for the wisdom of our faith.

Sometimes the poets can come to our help, those naïve dreamers who habitually see what others habitually miss. Joseph Mary Plunkett, who was executed in 1916 along with Padraig Pearse and Thomas MacDonagh, wrote:

I see his blood upon the rose
And in the stars the glory of his eyes,

His body gleams amid eternal snows,
His tears fall from the skies.[1]

May we, too, have not just eyesight but insight, so that we might see the Lord's handiwork around us. May we take strength and hope from the conviction that '*through him all things were made*'.

---

1. Joseph Mary Plunkett, 'I See His Blood Upon the Rose', *The Oxford Book of English Mystical Verse*, Nicholson & Lee, eds. (Oxford: Clarendon Press, 1917), p. 561.

For Us Men and for Our Salvation He Came Down from Heaven

Jesus is 'for us'. The Creed makes this very clear. In fact, the Creed makes two things about God very clear. On the one hand, God is all-powerful, the creator, the eternal, the source of all light and goodness. On the other hand, in Jesus, God has come to us, lived like us, shared our existence. By nature, God is infinite, heavenly, beyond us; but by his kindness God is with us and among us. The Creed captures this by saying that for us, Jesus 'came down from heaven'.

If you want to help someone who has fallen, you have to reach down; if you stay proud and tall, you may be proving your strength, your physical superiority, but you will be no use at all to the unfortunate person on the ground. That image can explain a great deal about Jesus: he is the one who has reached down to the fallen. Jesus has not asserted himself, he has not stood proud and tall, but has let go of his strength and greatness in order to enter our weakness and vulnerability.

Jesus is not simply a nice person who has done us a good turn: the Creed tells us plainly that he has come 'for our salvation'. Christ came to save us – not to affirm us. Yes, we need to be saved. This is a core truth of our Christian faith. To be a Christian is to acknowledge the power of God in Christ; it is also to acknowledge the power of sin in us. We cannot straighten ourselves out – we need outside intervention. Saint Paul puts the matter very plainly in his letter to the Romans: 'Since all have sinned and fall short of the glory of God, they are justified by his grace as a gift' (Rm 3:23). In other words, we have a deeply ingrained capacity for falling short in so many ways, for messing things up; but God puts things to rights, and offers us his help (the biblical name for God's help is 'grace') so that we might live well.

Does it seem a bit negative to insist on the universality of sinfulness and brokenness? Not if we give the matter some thought. If human weakness is universal, to the point that we need to be saved, bailed out, then this means that there is no perfect programme, no perfect politics, no perfect system or philosophy waiting to save us. And this, in turn, means that we do not owe total obedience to any organisation, any government, any political system.

One of the more ill-informed criticisms of Christian faith is that it makes believers gullible, ready to believe in anything. In fact, the opposite is true: believers in Christ are radically sceptical of all purely human efforts to save humanity. When all is said and done, believers look to God for salvation. Yes, they roll up their sleeves and work for the betterment of the world, but they know that only God can put reality completely to rights.

There is great freedom in this belief: it means that we are beholden to God alone. The belief that all people are in need of salvation means that we do not regard anyone in this world as a saviour, and we look with suspicion on anyone who is beginning to pose as one. Properly understood, the insistence that all men and women are sinners in need of salvation can be a bulwark against political tyranny of all kinds. As one writer wisely puts it:

> We have nothing to fear from those who do or do not believe in God; we have much to fear from those who do not believe in sin. The concept of sin is a stark acknowledgment that we can never be omnipotent, that we are bound and limited by human flaws and self-interest. The concept of sin is a check on the utopian dreams of a perfect world.[1]

If the belief that no human person is perfect puts a break on grand political dreams, on a personal level, the same belief can help us to be more realistic about ourselves, our families, our workmates, our neighbours. Sure, let us expect standards – and in high places let us expect high standards. But our Christian faith does not allow us to be tyrannical in our expectations, because it insists that we all need that bailout; it insists that the Lord came 'for our salvation'. Who is my neighbour, my child, my colleague, my friend? Someone who, like me, needs to be saved.

'For us men and for our salvation/he came down from heaven.' We need more than a bit of good advice, a tweaking here and there, a new political programme. We need salvation. Men and women of good will can achieve some great things, but only Christ can save us. Far from taking from our human dignity, this belief can prevent us

---

1. Chris Hedges, *I Don't Believe in Atheists* (London: Continuum, 2008), pp. 12–13.

from being enslaved by the latest notion (and there will always be a latest notion!) of what it is we need. It is Christ that we need, and we begin to find true freedom when we realise this need.

And by the Holy Spirit was Incarnate of the Virgin Mary

Several lines of the Creed describe the Holy Spirit and how the Spirit works. We will get to them in due course, but what we need to keep in mind for now is that when God does great things, it is God's Holy Spirit that is at work. The greatest thing of all was the coming of Christ, his taking human nature and living a human life; and it was God's Holy Spirit, rather than a human father, that brought this to pass.

Some people get hung up on the idea that Mary, a virgin, gave birth to Jesus without the involvement of a human father. They say that this is simply impossible. And of course, they are right: from a purely human perspective it is impossible. It is impossible that God should be born a helpless infant; it is impossible that the dead should rise; it is impossible that the deaf should hear and the blind see; that those who are in despair should be filled with hope. Many things are impossible.

What did Mary herself say when the angel Gabriel announced God's plan to her? She asked the angel: 'How can this be?' And the angel answered her: 'Nothing is impossible to God.' One of the great blessings of our Christian faith is that it does not leave us walled in by our circumstances, but gives us a hope that reaches beyond what is humanly possible.

The Creed tells us that it was by the Holy Spirit that Christ, who was already the Son of God, at a certain time became the Son of a human mother. Christ was *incarnate*, the Creed tells us; that word means simply that Christ took flesh, that he took on a *carnal* human nature.

Mary said 'yes' to God's plan. The best things happen when people say 'yes', when they agree to take part, to offer themselves and their energies. There is no social or political programme, no plan for renewal, that can bring real blessings, unless there are people behind it who are willing to say 'yes', to be available, to offer time, talents, concern.

Mary is above all the woman who made herself available to God, and that made all the difference. One of the earliest Christian theologians said that Mary conceived God's word in her heart before she conceived in her womb. And this is precisely where she is the great model for believers: in her openness to God. It follows that the only authentic devotion to Mary is the one that leads us to be more open to God. Imitation is the sincerest form of flattery!

Here is the whole drama of Mary in just three points. First, Mary shows us that the point of discipleship is to receive the Lord into our lives. Second, she shows us that this can involve real upheaval and suffering. What happened after Mary said her 'yes' to God's plan? Her relationship with Joseph practically broke down – he wanted to end their engagement. Not all that surprising, when he found out that his future wife was expecting a baby! All sorts of misunderstandings can arise when people allow Christ to enter their lives.

How did Mary deal with this crisis? This is the third point: Mary did not despair, or panic, or run away. She trusted in God. That was the crisis at the beginning of Christ's life. An even greater one came at the end. Mary's hands cradled an infant at the first Christmas, her eyes looked at her newborn with great love. Years later, the same hands received a lifeless body from the cross; the same eyes looked on, with unmeasured grief. So whatever else we might think, let us not imagine that Mary lived in a garden of roses, nor that her existence was all sweetness and light. There is a certain kind of piety that might suggest that. It may be a well-meaning piety, but it is blind to the human strength of Mary, the mother of Jesus.

We, as disciples, are called to conceive Christ in our hearts; to bring him into our families, our communities, our workplaces. This is what discipleship is. If we are not doing that, or trying, in some way, to do it, then our discipleship is at best defective. If disciples, like Mary, are called to be open to what God is doing, we also need Mary's steeliness: we need to be able to resist temptations to quit, to despair, to walk away. Mary followed her Son – even as he went through opposition, defeat and disfigurement. It might well be that a real mark of discipleship today is the willingness to continue following Christ, even when his image is disfigured by sin and derided by opposition.

May we be helped in that by the example of Mary; may we be supported by her prayers.

And Became Man

'What is man, that you are mindful of him?' (Ps 8:4). What is the human person? What is our life for? Where have we come from? Where are we going? The culture we inhabit does not offer answers to questions like these – in fact, it studiously avoids them. It prescribes our behaviour in ever-increasing detail, but it hasn't a clue what all that detail is finally for. Never have we been handed down so many directives; never have we been so lacking in a sense of direction. Because our culture has no answers to deep questions, it would rather we remain superficial, distracted, flitting like butterflies from one experience to the next.

When we are younger, quite naturally we want to have lots of new experiences; we want to jump into life and taste it to the full. But sooner or later, most people will begin to wonder who the person having all those experiences actually is: Who am I and what is my life for?

The Creed tells us that in Jesus, God took on our human nature completely: he *became man*. The *Catechism of the Catholic Church* tells us that it is only in the mystery of Jesus, the Word made flesh, that the mystery of our human nature becomes clear.[1] Our faith offers us the priceless

---

1. *Catechism of the Catholic Church* (Dublin: Veritas–Libreria Editrice Vaticana, 1994), 401.

gift of a clear understanding of our own humanity. It does not spoon-feed us; it does not offer ready-made answers to painful questions, but our faith *does* assure us that we are not random atoms in a random universe. Our life is precious, and it is meaningful.

In 1979, when Saint John Paul II addressed the young people of Ireland, he listed various ways in which people seek happiness. He mentioned drugs, materialism, sexual irresponsibility – and then he went on to speak some powerful words that show the great gift that faith has to offer:

> Something else is needed, something that you will find only in Christ, for he alone is the measure and the scale that you must use to evaluate your own life. In Christ, you will discover the true greatness of your own humanity; he will make you understand your own dignity as human beings 'created in the image and likeness of God'.

Today, there is more talk than ever about dignity, but there is no scale against which to measure it. 'Dignity' risks becoming an empty word or a political banner.

Saint John Paul never courted popularity; he never sought to sugar-coat the demands of discipleship, and on that occasion he went on say: 'Yes, Christ calls you, but he calls you in truth. His call is demanding, because he invites you to let yourselves be "captured" by him completely, so that your whole lives will be seen in a different light.'

Without that 'different light', as Pope John Paul well knew, we are like a dog in a cage at the airport who has chewed off the identification tag. There is no information about him: nobody knows his name, or his master's name, or where he has arrived from, or what his destination is.[2] He is a dog in the dark: he has no identity, no past, no future.

Just what is the light that Christ sheds on our human nature? Let us briefly consider five things that our faith teaches us about ourselves. For a start, we need not suffer the fate of that poor dog, because unlike it, we are capable of *self-knowledge*. We have hearts that are restless, and that ask big questions (the very kind of questions that our culture has no idea how to answer, and that invites us to treat with large doses of entertainment and pleasure). Our questions are an invitation to self-knowledge, to go deeper, not to be content with an endless stream of novelty or entertainment, not to anaesthetise ourselves with cheap pleasures.

In addition to self-knowledge, we are called to *self-possession*, to be masters of ourselves and our urges, rather than be mastered by them. This call to self-possession is the principal reason why Christian faith will never be flavour of the month with a culture that thinks that freedom is being able to do what I want, when I want. But without self-possession, what good are we? What use am I to an employer, if I do not possess myself enough to get up every day for work? What good am I to my spouse, if I do not possess myself enough to be faithful?

And after self-possession? When I possess myself, what comes next? I give myself away! This is a core Christian conviction regarding human nature: we become truly free by restraining ourselves, possessing ourselves, and then by giving ourselves away. We are designed for *self-giving*.

---

2. Peter Kreeft, *The Philosophy of Jesus* (South Bend, IN: St Augustine's Press, 2007), p. 78.

Surely we can all see that those who become caught up in the pursuit of immediate pleasure, immediate satisfaction, are unable to give themselves – and to the extent that they are unable to give themselves, they are unable to love.

Know yourself, possess yourself and you'll make a great lover. This is core Christian teaching. It is the very opposite of what our culture understands. Our faith then takes us a couple of steps further. It insists that we are made for *communion* with others; that we are called to be people of social concern, who work for the good of our community, our country and our world. Finally, our faith tells us that human nature is ultimately geared towards God, and that it is only in God that we can finally come to rest.

In a nutshell, what does our faith in Christ tell us about our human nature, which he shared? We are called to *know* ourselves, to *possess* ourselves, to *give* ourselves, to be *people of communion*, and to *seek God*. This is a truly great plan for any person's life.

For Our Sake He was Crucified Under Pontius Pilate

We are now at the heart of the Creed, where we profess what Christ has done '[f]or our sake'. In a sense, the entire Creed is about *relationships*: the relationship in the Trinity between Father, Son and Spirit; the relationship between God and creation; the relationship between God and us; the relationship among ourselves, as members of the Church. Here, at the centre of the Creed, we are considering the relationship between God and humanity, and that relationship has a name: Jesus.

The relationship between God and humanity is fully expressed in the crucifixion of Jesus. From God's perspective, the crucifixion and death of Jesus shows that God placed himself in humanity's hands; from the perspective of humanity, what was inflicted on Jesus shows the depths of rebellion and cruelty that we are capable of.

Let us consider the three phrases – 'For our sake', 'he was crucified', 'under Pontius Pilate' – in reverse order. The Creed reminds us that Lord was crucified 'under Pontius Pilate'. Aside from Jesus, there are just two people mentioned by name in the Creed: one is Mary, whose self-giving generosity gave Jesus life; the other is Pilate, whose self-serving politics gave Jesus death. To be a disciple is to be caught up in this ongoing drama that has Jesus at its centre. Will I be Mary? Or will I be Pilate?

Jesus lived in a country that was occupied by a foreign power, and Pontius Pilate was the senior official of the occupying force. But why does the Creed immortalise the memory of Pilate, a regional Roman official with a widespread reputation for cruelty? Because Jesus lived and died as a concrete individual, in a particular place, at a particular time, under a particular regime. God's plan was not vague or general, but was tied up in the details of time, place and politics.

That was how it was then; that is how it is now. God works in specific, concrete details – the details of our lives. And God's plan does not unfold only through the pleasant details: Pilate was anything but a pleasant detail, yet his cruelty and political ambition, though clearly at odds with God's will, were woven into the tapestry of God's providence. At the trial of Jesus, Pilate showed himself to be more interested in keeping in the good books of the Emperor of Rome than in seeking the truth of the God of heaven. Yet, by God's providence, this self-serving man served God's plan, to the extent that Pilate is now a permanent footnote in the history of our salvation.

Pilate sentenced Jesus to be crucified. The Romans had different forms of capital punishment, depending on the offence being punished, and crucifixion was regarded as the most depraved and degrading form of all. It was not simply a means of execution – it was a statement. It said: 'Here is what happens to the enemies of the Empire.' The purpose of crucifixion was not merely to kill someone, but to put them on display for all to see. But in the case of Jesus, what was on display was God's love for humanity.

To be crucified by the Roman authorities was to be eliminated, crushed by the most powerful political and military force the world had yet seen. To be crucified was to be rendered completely powerless. In the Creed, there is a huge contrast between the words 'through him all things were made' and the words 'he was crucified'. Jesus is God; he is all-powerful. Yet he subjected himself to complete powerlessness. Why?

This brings us to the first of those three phrases: 'For our sake'. Why did Jesus, who is 'God from God' and through whom 'all things were made' die on a Roman cross? Surely the all-powerful Lord could have chosen some other way? Saints and scholars have rightly been uneasy with the idea that the sufferings of Jesus were the price demanded by an angry God if sinful humanity was to be saved, and to a great extent the cross must remain a mystery. That said, it is possible for us to grasp something of the logic of God's choice of radical powerlessness.

If we consider the matter, what is the most that power can achieve in restoring a broken relationship? If someone inflicts great damage on me, I can have recourse to law, and have an offender's behaviour restrained, whether by imprisonment or some other sanction. But this proper and necessary exercise of power does not reach into the heart of the offender – it does not, of itself, lead to repentance; it does not, of itself, restore the *relationship* between offender and offended.

In willingly submitting to the powerlessness of crucifixion, the all-powerful God was saying: 'I want something more than justice! I don't just want to restrain the sinfulness of humanity, I want to restore my relationship of love with them. And in order to do this, I will not coerce, I will not exercise the power that I possess, but seek to reach right into people's hearts.'

The crucified Jesus teaches us this above all: God's desire is not so much to *restrain* us as to *restore* us to full relationship with him. And to this end, he sets his power aside, and appeals to our hearts.

He Suffered Death and was Buried

We are used to the cross. We hang it on the walls of churches, homes and schools; some of us wear it around our necks, sometimes merely as an item of jewellery. It is easy to forget that the cross is an instrument of capital punishment, and that we might just as well display a little replica of an electric chair, or a hangman's noose. We should never forget that the cross was not a pretence – Jesus died on it.

Both historians and medical doctors have studied crucifixion in detail, and their combined disciplines tell us that when people were crucified, the immediate cause of death was not blood loss but asphyxiation. Crucifixion did not damage any vital organs; victims remained fully conscious; but as they gradually tired and weakened, they became unable to bear their own weight, and so they sagged on their cross, with their outstretched arms bearing more and more of the weight of their body. This put increasing pressure on their diaphragm and hence on their breathing, until eventually, and very slowly, they asphyxiated. It was fully expected that crucifixion would lead to a slow, horrible and terrifying death. In the case of Jesus, there seems to have been some surprise at how quickly he died.

The Gospel of John (19:33) makes a point of remarking that when some Roman soldiers went to finish Jesus off by breaking his legs, they found that he was already dead.

'He suffered death,' the Creed tells us, before it adds the words, 'and was buried.' Have you ever wondered why this should be specified? In the climate of Palestine, as is still the case in many parts of the world, burial was a matter of urgency – the dead were buried as a matter of course and as quickly as possible, before decay and putrefaction set in. Why, then, should the Creed spell out the fact that Jesus was buried, when this was taken for granted, as the universal practice?

The Creed does this to underline the fact that Jesus had died. He hadn't simply passed out, only to revive later on; his body hadn't been stolen by his disciples, so that they could invent the myth that he had risen from the dead. This was exactly what the enemies of Jesus feared: that his followers would steal his body. That was why they went to Pilate to ask that Jesus' tomb be secured to prevent his body being removed (cf. Mt 27:62-66). Even after they had killed him, Jesus' enemies were going out of their way to silence him! *Silence the message!* That has been the principal tactic and strategy of the enemies of Christ since the very beginning.

So yes, Jesus died and was buried, and his burial place, a borrowed tomb, was sealed by a rock. We believe that Jesus did not remain dead; we believe in the resurrection. But our faith is insistent – and the Creed spells this out – that there was a time when Jesus was dead. His lifeless body, taken down from the cross, was left in a tomb, which was sealed and had a military guard stationed outside – and that was no guard of honour!

'Christ is alive', so the Easter hymn goes; Christ was dead, so the Creed insists. There was a time in the history of the world when the Son of God lay dead in a tomb. Now, Christ is alive, his tomb is empty; but the world remains full of occupied tombs. Tombs and graves where loved ones lie; tombs of illness, anxiety, addiction, despair, scandal, hurt. The fact that Christ once lay lifeless in the tomb holds out a powerful message of hope to all those who are acquainted with tombs. The Lord has been there.

In our liturgy, that time when the Lord lay silent in the tomb is re-lived each year on Holy Saturday. This is the day between Christ's death on Good Friday, and his resurrection on Easter Sunday. In many ways, we are called to be Holy Saturday people. We haven't personally experienced the resurrection – our departed loved ones have not been restored to us; the world remains a broken place. But we believe that Christ has made the journey in full, from life, to the cross, to the tomb, and back to life.

A core challenge of discipleship is that we wait faithfully at whatever tombs life presents, and that we keep faith with others in their time of need. Christians are people who neither run from the tragedies of life, nor provide glib answers to them. We are people who have faith in Christ, this Lord of ours who knows the tomb from the inside. It is this faith that enables us to live our Holy Saturdays, with real suffering, perhaps, but without despair.

What shields us from despair is the conviction that he, the master, has been there. He, the Lord: 'he suffered death and was buried'. He is with us in all our Holy Saturdays, those times when we have tasted death, but not yet tasted resurrection.

And Rose Again on the Third Day

Why do people leave the Church? For various reasons, among the more obvious of which are scandal and disillusionment. In addition to asking why people leave, we would do well to ask why they joined to begin with. More specifically, we might ask why, at the very beginning of the Church, people joined it in droves. At the time of the earliest Christians, there was a great variety of religions that people could subscribe to, with all sorts of philosophies and outlooks, some of which offered a great deal of wisdom and commonsense.

Christianity, too, offered wisdom, but it was a stern religion, one that made great demands of its adherents. Wherever its attraction lay, it certainly was not an easier option for people who were tired of the demands of paganism. Yet people flocked to the new faith, and to the Church, in great numbers. What was the attraction? What did people see in this faith that so many people today no longer see? What was it that fascinated them, to the extent that many of them were willing to face martyrdom rather than return to their old, pre-Christian ways?

Many of the earliest records make it clear that countless early Christians were happy with life, yet unafraid of suffering and death. Today, many people seem unhappy with life, yet terribly afraid of suffering and death. G. K. Chesterton once noted that there is a certain sadness about that that calls for a new kind of prophet: not like the early prophets, who reminded people that they were going to die, but who would, instead, remind people that they are not dead yet.[1]

What was the difference between those earliest Christians, and many believers today? The heart of the matter is that the earliest Christians believed that Jesus Christ was real, that he was alive. They believed that, as a matter of concrete fact, he had risen from the dead. They did not believe that, as a matter of psychological or sentimental fact, he was somehow living on in their hearts. The earliest Christians believed that the Lord had risen from the dead. This was the big bang – the energy at the very beginning of the faith: 'He is risen!' These were the words spoken by the very first witnesses, who ran off and told others that they had seen the Lord.

From the beginning, there have been attempts to debunk and disprove the resurrection of Jesus, to put it all down to hallucinations, or deception, or wishful thinking. Those attempts are as old as the Church; up to our own time, hardly an Easter goes by without the publication of some new book that is allegedly going to sound the death-knell for Christian faith. 'Easter is cancelled: they've found the tomb, and there are bones in it!'

The first Christians were drawn to the new faith – in many cases drawn away from culturally enriching practices – because they were convinced that Jesus Christ was alive. This was the heart of the matter then, and it is the heart of

---

1. Cf. Philip Yancey, 'G. K. Chesterton, Prophet of Mirth', *Orthodoxy*, G. K. Chesterton (New York: Doubleday/Image, 2001), p. xxi.

the matter now: he 'rose again'! The gospels are careful to insist that after he rose from the dead, Jesus was seen. He was seen by many people, beginning with the women who had made their way to his tomb, hoping to get a last look at a dead body.

What about today when many people looking at the Church imagine they are taking a last look at a dying body? What is to become in our time of the faith that took hold of countless pagans, and turned them into fearless disciples of Christ and dedicated members of his Church? Today, we need to return to those words from the Creed – he 'rose again'. Christ is alive, and this is why, in spite of sadness, scandal and strife, the Church is still in business. Indeed, the Church has no other business than to proclaim Christ to the world, both in words and in deeds. To the extent that our faith is jaded, to the extent that we are bored or cynical, we need to return to that cornerstone conviction, to the big bang that is at the origin of the universe of Christian faith: Christ, who died, has risen. Christ is alive and he is real.

The Creed tells us that Christ rose again 'on the third day'. Day one was Good Friday, the day of his death; on day two, he lay in the tomb; on day three, he rose from the dead. Remember that as a child, Jesus was lost in the Temple, to be found on the third day. We cannot compress all of life's mishaps and tragedies into a three-day schedule, but in those words, the Creed tells us that the time of death's victory is limited by God's plan. God has imposed a limit on every manifestation of evil. For every experience of betrayal, suffering and death, there is, in God's providence, a 'third day'. The Christ who, in human weakness, 'suffered death and was buried' is the Christ who, by God's power, 'rose again on the third day'.

In Accordance with the Scriptures

The story of the two weary disciples on the road to Emmaus is one of the loveliest incidents in the Gospel (cf. Luke 24). These are two very sad individuals: the hopes they had invested in Jesus have been shattered; he has been crucified and buried. The story is over. The rock rolled across the entrance to the tomb is, as far as they are concerned, like a great, cosmic full stop.

Ironically, they are walking away from Jerusalem on the first Easter Sunday. As they go, Jesus joins them. Even though they do not recognise him, they engage him in conversation; they open up to him and tell him how their hopes have been disappointed. At a certain point in the conversation, Jesus says to them: 'Was it not necessary that the Christ should suffer these things …' Jesus then goes on to point out how the scriptures had foretold what was to happen to the Christ. Later that day, speaking to another group of disciples, Jesus, the gospel tells us, 'opened their minds to understand the scriptures' (Lk 24:45).

In effect, what Jesus is saying to these groups of disciples on the first Easter Sunday is something like this: 'You have been deeply shocked, saddened. You have reached what looks like the end of the road, an impenetrable barrier. But hear this: unseen by you, God has been working through these deeply painful events. He has been ahead of events all along, guiding and leading. What looks like the end of your plans has been in accordance with God's plan.'

This is the meaning of that lovely biblical phrase which we pray in the Creed: 'in accordance with the Scriptures' (cf. 1 Cor 15:3). What happened to Jesus was not a failure but a fulfilment.

The very first homily preached in the Church, St Peter's Pentecost Day sermon, makes this point even more starkly. Peter stood up on Pentecost day and said to a crowd of people in Jerusalem: 'This Jesus, delivered up according to the definite plan and foreknowledge of God, you crucified and killed by the hands of lawless men. But God raised him up' (Acts 2:23-24). Here, Peter tells us that all that had happened, even the disastrous events of Good Friday, had been embraced by God's providence.

Let us be clear: there is no simple route for any of us through the difficulties and tragedies that life can throw at us and at our loved ones. Faith does not offer simple routes – it offers the assurance that the most twisted and tragic itinerary can be embraced by God's plan, and it calls us to do our best to make this world a better place. God's embrace of all our circumstances has a very specific name, and that name is *providence*. God's providence means that reality does not run away from him, no matter how far or how chaotically it may run away from us.

God's providence means that he is able to write all events into his plan. In this, God has been compared to the conductor of an orchestra in which a key musician has played a glaring bum note. The note is so terribly discordant it could cause the whole symphony to unravel, but the conductor is so brilliant he simply conducts around it, and the mistake gets absorbed into the score.

That is God's providence: his infinite capacity to absorb error, sin and tragedy. How often we would rather that God should write these things out of the script in advance, so that we could live in a world free of tragedy. But this is not the world we live in. It is not the world Jesus lived in. Our faith is not founded on a pipe dream that offers some kind of free pass through life. It is, rather, founded on the conviction that the greatest evil ever, the torture and murder of Jesus, was 'in accordance with the Scriptures', fully part of God's plan.

There is a misunderstanding waiting in the wings, a serious misunderstanding, one that has caused untold misery for Christian believers. If all that happens is part of God's plan, does that mean that the dice have been cast and there is nothing we can do? Far from it! That everything is 'in accordance with the Scriptures' means that God is so deeply present and at work in all that happens that nothing can finally derail his plans. God was at work in the agony and death of his only Son. Our faith holds out the hope that the same God is still at work when agony and death are doing their worst in our time. God has not destined or predestined any of us for destruction. His desire for our destiny is quite the opposite, as the Bible makes clear: 'He destined us on love to be his sons and daughters through Jesus Christ' (Eph 1:5). Jesus himself was completely convinced of this. It was because he believed in God's providence that Jesus could pray: 'Father, all things are possible to you; remove this cup from me; yet not what I will, but what you will' (Mk 14:36).

'In accordance with the Scriptures.' Properly understood, those words assure us that God's plan embraces all events – from the loveliest to the most awful. May we find peace and hope in that assurance; may it give us the encouragement to become more engaged with the sufferings and needs of our time.

He Ascended into Heaven

When Jesus had finished his earthly life and work, he departed from his followers; he no longer walked and talked with them. Their discipleship entered a new phase; in fact they became like us: they walked by faith and not by sight. Two questions can help us to reflect on the departure of Jesus, his ascension into heaven: What did he bring with him? What did he leave behind? These questions can prove very relevant to us, as we try to live out our faith in this Lord whom we believe, but don't see.

What did Jesus bring with him when he left his disciples? He went to heaven, the Creed tells us, he went into the presence of God the Father, but he did not go empty-handed. First of all, Jesus brought our human nature with him. He had lived a fully human life, with the ups and downs, the limitations and aspirations, of a flesh-and-blood person in the confines of time and space. This is life that Jesus brings to the Father as he ascends into heaven.

Here, it might help if we use our imagination and ask what God the Father saw when Jesus ascended into heaven and took up his place at God's side. In Jesus, God saw a human nature that he loved; he saw everything that he desired for each one of his children. In the human nature of Jesus, God the Father saw his dream for every man and woman. In Jesus, God saw and sees and loves our humanity, our concerns, our struggles.

But Jesus brought something else with him: 'When he ascended on high, he took captivity captive' (Eph 4:8). That means, quite simply, that anything that enslaves humanity, anything that defeats us, anything that would make us captive, has itself been defeated, captured, by Jesus. While we continue to experience their effects, we are no longer captive to sin, death and despair, because the Lord has dealt with them.

What Jesus brought with him, then, was our human nature, untainted and free; along with sin and death, bound up in chains. This starts to become very concrete if we think about the world we live in. Don't many people, at least at certain times, experience life as a burden, a kind of captivity? And don't sin and death appear, at least at certain times, to have a free hand in this broken world of ours? But Jesus has reversed this: in him, it is human nature that has been set free, and everything that burdens it that has been taken captive. This state of affairs has been established by Jesus, set up in the heavens. And this, for us, is a hope that helps us to live this life, here and now, to the full.

What did Jesus leave behind him? When the Lord departed from his earliest followers, he left a *task* and a *promise*. The task was 'Go and make disciples of all nations' (Mt 28:19). This was an enormous, universal task. Jesus did not say, 'Go and teach people their prayers; go and instruct them in such and such a practice.' He was vastly more ambitious for humanity: he wanted his followers to make nations into disciples!

The Lord's final ambition and plan is to bring the whole world where he has gone, to lead humanity after him. Could the Lord really be looking at the world today and saying to his followers: 'Go and make disciples of the nations'? Or was that message just for a time, a time that has now expired? There is no evidence in anything the Lord said that his intention was to make disciples of some generations, but not of others. For that matter, there has never been a perfect generation of disciples; each generation brings its own challenges – sometimes very great challenges.

The Lord's parting wish is for the making of disciples; the times we live in seem geared more to the unmaking of disciples. Is there anything we can do? Will opposition, cynicism, indifference and discouragement prove the Lord to have been a naïve optimist? We do not, of course, know how things will unfold; we are living through a time of ongoing upheaval. For that reason, we need to be more aware than ever of the second thing the Lord left behind: along with the task, he left a promise: 'I am with you always, to the end of the age' (Mt 28:20).

We do not know the future, but we can be sure of this much: the only way to future-proof our discipleship is to be people who lean on the Lord's promise to be with us. Without that conviction, all the plans and projects in the world will not lead to renewal. 'I am with you always, to the end of the age.' Let us find confidence in those words, a confidence that might enable us to pray:

God is for us a refuge and strength
A helper close at hand, in time of distress:
So we shall not fear though the earth should rock,
Though the mountains fall into the depths of the sea.
(Ps 46:1-2)

And is Seated at the Right Hand of the Father

Begrudgery is something at which it is said Irish people excel. It comes in various shades, but most broadly, it is the attitude that nobody should be allowed to rise too high, and that if they do so, they need to be taken down a peg or two, in order that they be kept in touch with their humble origins. I have often thought that Irish begrudgery is the exact opposite of the American Dream. The latter is the naïve expectation that anyone can do well if they apply themselves; the former is the cynical insistence that nobody should be allowed to do all that well.

Every time has its characteristic oddness and blindness. One of the oddities of our time is that many people manage to combine an almost worshipful interest in celebrity with a deep cynicism towards anyone who appears to be outstandingly good and authentic. It is almost as if we were saying, 'Lots of glitzy trash, please, but none of the real McCoy.' Somehow, we have learned to be fascinated with anger, stupidity and infidelity, and at the same time we have acquired a deep mistrust of those who appear to be wholesome and wise.

As Christians, we are blessed to have a way of cutting through the cynicism of our time, rather like a compass that will guide us through the fog. Our compass, our guide, is Jesus Christ, this person who lived a fully human life, and who is now, as the Creed tells us, 'seated at the right hand of the Father'. Those words tell us that Jesus is no longer a hidden figure, walking the roads of an insignificant corner of the world, with a small group of peasants for followers. That Jesus is seated at the right hand of the Father means that he is now *recognised* for who and what he is.

Jesus, the Creed tells us, is seated. In the culture which gave us the Creed, to be seated was a sign of honour; it was also a sign of authority. In early Christian art, Jesus is sometimes depicted as seated or enthroned, in the manner of a king surrounded by his subjects. Some of this art was a very deliberate 'copyright theft': it was based upon depictions of the Roman emperor, and in effect it proclaimed that it was now to Christ, rather than to Caesar, that Christians gave their homage. And so there is (yet another) political statement in the heart of the Creed: to be a Christian is to look to Christ as our final authority, and to be radically sceptical of anyone who might claim a higher authority. There is, as it happens, a characteristic kind of Christian scepticism, and this is exactly what it is reserved for.

The Creed tells us that Jesus is seated *at the right hand* of God. In biblical language, to be seated at a king's right hand was to be given the highest possible honour and power. The phrase 'the right hand of God' was a kind of shorthand for God's power and governance; to have access to this power was to share in it.

In early Christian art, when Jesus is depicted at seated, he very often has a book on his lap, open on some words of Scripture which he is inviting us to put into practice. At other times, he is pictured as handing a scroll to St Peter or another disciple, just as the Roman emperor would have handed a decree to one of his senior officials, so that it could be implemented. Like the Roman emperor, the seated Christ gives guidance and instruction, but unlike the emperor, he does not use force to ensure that his commands are perfectly carried out.

That little bit of background to those words of the Creed might raise some questions for us. Do I look to Christ for guidance? Do I defer to his authority? Do I seek to allow him to shape my life, rather than being drawn or driven by fad or fancy? The Lord who is seated at the right hand of the Father is our reference point, and he is a gentle Lord, who appeals but does not impose.

Back for a moment to the scepticism of our times. There is, as I have said, a kind of healthy Christian scepticism, one that allows us to see through a lot of this world's nonsense. But there is also a general, unhealthy scepticism towards a lot of what is good and wholesome. We are blessed to have a tonic for this attitude. Our tonic is honour and worship of Christ. Christ is indeed our friend, but we should be wary of any notion that he is simply our buddy. He is far more than that; he is, in his own words, 'the way, the truth and the life' (Jn 14:6).

A true sense of honour and respect towards Christ the Lord is not beneath our dignity; quite the opposite, it is an expression of our dignity. No loyal subject every felt slighted at the prospect of offering homage to a beloved king. No Christian should ever hesitate to offer genuine homage and honour to Christ, who is our guide, our reference point, our final authority. He is 'seated at the right hand of the Father'. May he be enthroned in our hearts and our lives.

He Will Come Again in Glory

One of the criticisms occasionally levelled against our Christian faith is that it distracts people from the here and now. If we are focused on the future, can we be focused on the present? The American philosopher, Henry David Thoreau, when asked if he believed in an afterlife, famously answered: 'One world at a time.'

Our faith invites us to be mindful of the future, of that moment when, as the Creed tells us, Christ will come again. Does this mean that our faith is a distraction from what is going on in the present? To answer this question, we need only consider how people tend to behave when they are expecting someone. What about the woman who is expecting a baby? Or the family who are looking forward to the visit of a much-loved relative they haven't seen for a long time? Far from *distracting* people in their day-to-day living, their looking forward *focuses* them: their life becomes a getting ready; every new day brings things to do, preparations to be made; there is anticipation and excitement.

We might also think about the opposite situation, where people slip into the kind of depression that robs them of any sense that there are good things to come. This does not have the effect of focussing their attention more clearly on the present: quite the opposite, people who feel they have nothing to look forward to can be quite unable to focus on the present. To be healthily human is to look forward, to have a sense that life is bringing something else, something new; that our reality is not all flat and exhausted. If, for whatever reason, we have no sense of any goodness ahead, we may be heading for trouble. Indeed, psychologists tell us that one of the difficulties faced by people who have experienced deep trauma is the absence of a sense of the future, an abiding feeling that there is nothing to look forward to.

Our faith crowns this psychological insight by telling us that no matter what our past holds, whatever sufferings we have experienced or sins we have committed, we are offered a future. As the saying goes, every saint has a past, and every sinner has a future. The world can be a cruel place; some people suffer very greatly. Our faith does not gloss over the hard edges of life, but it assures us that ultimately, the future lies in God's hands. Christ 'will come again'. He is the Lord of the future, who at some point will come in glory, and who, in the meantime, wants to enter our lives in more ordinary ways.

It is a blessed thing to live a life that has a direction, a life of readiness, of preparedness, a life with a purpose. Indeed, to live this kind of life is not only a blessing: it is a command. Jesus tells us: 'Keep watch, for you know not the day nor the hour' (Mt 25:13). One of the best ways to keep on our toes is to spend some time on our knees; to keep up some steady contact with the Lord who will come again.

A healthy exercise for us as believers is to compare what our faith offers with what a non-faith understanding offers.

There are many people – people we know and love, people with whom we work, we ourselves at certain times – for whom the future seems flat and dull. Our faith – this can never be stressed enough – does not candy-coat the hard realities of life, but it *does* offer a vision and a hope for our lives. In a lovely passage in the Old Testament, the Lord says through one of his prophets: 'I know the plans I have for you … plans for welfare and not for evil, to give you a future and a hope' (Jer 29:11).

Some people may say, 'What's the use of words like that when you are struggling to make ends meet, or when the test for illness comes back positive?' But what words will offer the hope that every human heart longs for? If we reject those words of faith, what words will we choose when we are up against it? Should we not, rather, say with Peter, 'Lord, to whom shall we go? You have the words of eternal life' (Jn 6:68).

'He will come again.' The next time we hear or read the suggestion that our faith is backward-looking, we might call to mind the fact that it is actually forward-looking. To be a Christian is to look forward. It is to look to the *future* with the kind of expectancy that makes us more attentive than ever to how we are living in the *present*.

The Creed states that Christ will come again 'in glory'. When he comes again, he will not turn up like an undocumented refugee, hoping to find a kindly reception. He will not have a hunted or beseeching look in his eyes. He will be seen by all for who and what he is: the one before whom, as St Paul writes, 'every knee shall bow … and every tongue confess that Jesus Christ is Lord' (Phil 2:10-11).

To Judge the Living and the Dead

Almost two hundred years ago, the Danish philosopher Søren Kierkegaard told a story which was intended to rattle the cages of his contemporaries, to shake people out of their smugness. His story speaks just as clearly today. It is the story of a fire that broke out in a crowded theatre: the fire started backstage and the clown came out on stage to warn the public. They thought this was great fun, and they applauded loudly. The clown repeated his warning; they applauded again. Pretty soon, they all died laughing. Kierkegaard reckoned that that was just how the world would end: to general applause from people who thought it was all a bit of a joke.

Perhaps that story is even more relevant to our day, given how much time and expense go into entertainment. Our culture has so conditioned us to expect to be entertained that we can even run the risk of expecting worship to be entertaining. Quite rightly, we expect that our minds and hearts will be engaged in our worship, but that is not the same thing as entertainment. At Mass, we commemorate Christ's self-giving death on Calvary for love of sinners; as we do so, we are not 'competing with television'! We will do well to be wary of the simple, 'either-or' formula: either it is entertaining, or it is boring.

Thank God for entertainment, for art and imagination, for a laugh and a smile. Yet our faith reminds us, and urges us to bear in mind, that life is serious. Our life is not a dress rehearsal; it is an unrepeatable journey, involving an ongoing exercise of our free will, at the end of which we will be judged according to how we have acted.

This fact of judgement is not a threat; it is an acknowledgment of our human dignity: how we act matters; our choices have consequences. We already know that this is a law of life: we see the consequences of good and evil actions all around us. Our faith insists that Christ, as our judge, will finally respect our choices. Those who would downplay or soft-peddle the notion of Christ's judgment do us no favours: they fail to respect the utter seriousness of our situation.

Does this mean we should live a life of fear and trembling? Are we to stop thinking of Jesus as a friend, or to replace his crown of thorns with a judge's wig? In fact, there are two common mistakes, two extremes we can fall into. One extreme is to ignore or deny the fact of judgement, to smile benevolently at the clown who insists on it. This is a common error in our day. The other extreme, no longer common, is to become so preoccupied with the Lord's judgement that we live a life of craven fear.

What does it mean to be a 'God-fearing' person? When that expression is used of someone, it does not mean they are a nervous wreck, but that they are upright, honourable, compassionate. Each of us is called to be God-fearing in the sense that we have a healthy awareness that God respects our freedom, and allows us to experience its consequences in this life and in eternity. There is an interesting line in the Book of Exodus, where Moses says to the people: 'Do not be afraid. God has come to test you, so that you may fear him, and not sin' (Ex 20:20).

Do not be afraid – fear God! To fear God is to respect reality; to know that the way in which we use our freedom has lasting consequences. When this is clear in our minds, we will strive to avoid sin; we will not treat life as a nursery game that we can leave behind us like a child dropping a toy. Genuine fear of God can help us to be less fearful in the face of life's challenges – and life's temptations; it teaches us a sane and healthy sense of the seriousness of life.

Here are three final thoughts on the fact that Christ will judge us, whether we are alive or dead when he comes. First, the fact of God's judgement does not entitle us to judge others. Let God judge others; let each of us examine his or her own conscience, rather than the consciences of our brothers or sisters. Second, Christ will judge us with mercy. If we try to live a life that is merciful, that seeks to forgive, that lets go of grudges, if we try to build bridges rather than walls, then we are opening ourselves up to the Lord's mercy. As the letter of St James puts it: 'Judgement is without mercy to the one who has shown no mercy; yet mercy triumphs over judgement' (Jas 2:13). Third, since it is Christ who is our merciful judge, we should never condemn ourselves. As long as we draw breath, we can breathe in the Lord's mercy. The words 'too late' are not a part of the Christian vocabulary.

And His Kingdom will Have No End

The culture we inhabit is generally open to religion – and it generally imposes a condition on that openness. It is happy for people to hold whatever beliefs they want, so long as they do not let those beliefs influence their behaviour in politics, business or education. In other words, the world we live in desires that faith and religion be something private.

As Christians, we collide with that desire every time we pray, as the Lord taught us: 'Thy kingdom come.' And the Creed insists that, whatever the exact details of this kingdom, it will be unending: 'his kingdom will have no end'. Contrary to what our culture understands and wants, there is no such thing as private Christianity. The practice of faith is about a whole lot more than attending church once a week: it is about living a life that brings God's values into this world, into its politics, its business, its education. We are called to be 'kingdom people' – people who, by the way we live our lives, make this world God's place, a place that is fertile with goodness, compassion, forgiveness, hope.

By the grace of God, we are already doing this in many ways. Let us never forget that every single thing we do for goodness' sake, all our striving for kindness and our efforts to persevere in our day-to-day commitments – all of these things are part of how God's kingdom comes about. We pray 'thy kingdom come,' and we try to live a life that makes that prayer a reality.

Our Christian faith is, of course, something deeply *personal*, but this does not mean it is *private*. Its effects should be seen in our world – and by God's grace are often plain to be seen. But if faith is to have a public impact, does this mean that the Church should be getting involved in politics, or seeking direct political influence? Not at all. History tells us that Church leaders can be just as corrupt and self-serving as leaders in any other walk of life. Our Christian faith is to have a public face; we are to claim this world for God. But this is not a party political manifesto. It means, rather, that our discipleship of Christ, when it is authentic, is not locked up in some private corner of our minds, but has a clear impact on the community and society in which we live.

I once heard it said of a politician: 'His religious beliefs are so private they don't even interfere with his own life.' There is also the story of the man who went to confession and did not mention his tax-dodging. When his wife questioned him about this, he said: 'I told the priest my sins, not my business!' Our Christian faith is to reach into all parts of our lives, and in that way to be a part of God's great project: the building of an eternal kingdom of love, justice and peace.

That might sound impossibly idealistic, so let us listen to the realism of Jesus. Jesus compared the kingdom to a field where wheat is sown, but someone with a grudge against the farmer added lots of weeds. One of the workers wanted to go and root out the weeds, but the farmer told him to leave the wheat and weeds together till harvest time, when it would be easier to tell them apart. Too much zeal in rooting out the weeds might only damage the wheat.

There is great human wisdom in this parable. Some people are very zealous – they want things to be sorted out straight away. Their motto is, 'If you want to make an omelette, you have to break some eggs'. In their holy zeal, they can be cruel to those around them, breaking hearts rather than eggs. They can discredit the very best of causes. The Lord teaches us that in this life, we have to accept limitations, sinfulness, shortsightedness, and that if we try too hard to root these out, we are liable to do more harm than good. God's kingdom calls us to commitment, not to crankiness.

Again, Jesus compares the kingdom to a tiny seed that grows into a very large plant. Don't so many of our efforts seem terribly small and ineffective? Yet the Lord says to us: 'Don't worry – the best things result from the smallest beginnings.' Look around you today: the biggest tree you will see started out as a tiny seed! As one writer puts it, our gallant efforts, however small they may be, are 'the currency of the kingdom'.

Or again, Jesus compares the kingdom of heaven to a woman putting a measure of yeast into a batch of dough. The yeast is hidden, but it causes the whole loaf to rise. In our word, there is a lot of highly visible evil: crime, scandal, violence. But there is also an untold amount of hidden goodness. It will, by God's providence, leaven the world.

Let us allow the wisdom of Jesus to give us hope and encouragement, as we try to live kingdom-lives. There will always be weeds among the wheat – problems and obstacles. We must live with that. Our efforts are often very puny, but no less important for that. A lot of what is good gets no attention, but there is more than enough goodness in the world to buoy us up in our efforts to live a life that says, 'Thy kingdom come'.

I Believe in the Holy Spirit

With these words, we begin the third 'chapter' of the Creed. We have already said, 'I believe in one God' and 'I believe in one Lord, Jesus Christ'. Now we have reached the part of the Creed devoted to the Third Person of the Trinity.

It is often said that the Holy Spirit is the forgotten person of the Trinity. If this is so, then the remedy is not so much for us to raise the Holy Spirit's profile – as if we could do such a thing – as to be more aware of how the Spirit acts in our lives. Theologians say that the Holy Spirit is 'self-effacing'. This term is used to remind us that the Spirit's work is to lead us to God. It is as if the Holy Spirit were saying, 'Don't look at me; look at God the Father, as he shows himself to us in Jesus his Son.'

The Creed will tell us something of who the Holy Spirit is, but for now, let us consider what the Spirit *does*. Jesus once compared the Holy Spirit to a blowing wind (cf. Jn 3:8), and indeed God's Spirit is the wind in the sails of the Church. Although she has been through many storms, the Church sometime seems to be motionless, stuck. An image from Coleridge's 'The Rime of the Ancient Mariner' fits well: 'As idle as a painted ship/Upon a painted ocean.'

With the wind apparently gone out of our sails, many people say that what we need is a new ship. But the gospel truth is that what we need is wind in our sails, and that wind is the Spirit of God, without whom no projects or changes will avail us. The first page in any chapter of renewal, whether in the Church or in our personal lives as believers, must be written by God's Holy Spirit. Once that is done, once we are in tune with the Spirit, we are in a position to ask about any structural or institutional changes that need to be made.

What does the Holy Spirit do, in our lives and in the life of the Church? To put it another way, what happens without the Spirit? First of all, without the Holy Spirit there is no real discipleship, and no real renewal. At the end of his earthly life, when Jesus was leaving his disciples, he said to them: 'Stay in the city until you are clothed with the power from on high' (Lk 24:49). Jesus did not want his followers even to attempt to proclaim the gospel until they had received the Holy Spirit.

Without the Holy Spirit, there are no new beginnings, only false starts. It is not a question of sitting back and letting the Holy Spirit do all the work. When we learn to depend on God's power, which is the power of the Holy Spirit, then we will work like never before, but we know that it is the Spirit who guides and crowns our efforts.

Without the Holy Spirit there is no lasting wisdom, there are no words of wisdom. Recall that at the first Pentecost, the Holy Spirit came to rest on the disciples in the form of tongues of fire. It is easy to generate chatter, but it is only by the power of the Spirit that we can generate language of meaning and hope.

There is a wonderful scene in the Acts of the Apostles, where Peter and John and a group of Christians are praying together in a time of persecution. The writer tells us: 'As they prayed, the house where they were assembled rocked; they were all filled with the Holy Spirit and began to proclaim the word of God' (Acts 4:31). Whatever else we might say about our Church and our way of worshipping, we can hardly say it rocks! We need the Spirit if our faith is to come to life.

Without the Holy Spirit, there is no real prayer. It is not that we must directly address the Holy Spirit every time we pray, but without the Spirit's power, we simply cannot pray; and whenever we *do* pray, it is thanks to the Spirit. As St Paul puts it: 'The Spirit helps us in our weakness, for we do not know how to pray as we ought' (Rm 8:26).

Our Christian faith calls us to live a life of love – a love that is not limited to our loved ones, but that reaches out into our community, our society, our world. How can we live a life of love in a world that wounds, a world that can be so cold and indifferent? Without the Holy Spirit, we cannot live a life that loves beyond natural human boundaries. With the help of the Spirit, things can be very different: we can discover, with St Paul, that 'the love of God has been poured into our hearts by the Holy Spirit which has been given us' (Rm 5:5).

Finally, the Holy Spirit does not simply confirm all our plans and our ideas; the Spirit who helps can also hinder. The earliest missionaries found that some of their best-laid plans met with failure (cf. Acts 16:6-7). Rather than becoming disillusioned, they saw the hand of God at work, and were confident that the Holy Spirit acted also through disappointment and deferral. Our efforts to walk with the Spirit do not bring automatic success: what they bring is the confidence that – to quote St Paul once more – 'in everything God works for good with those who love him, who are called according to his purpose' (Rm 8:28).

The Lord, the Giver of Life

A well-known Christian apologist asks the question: 'Why did twelve fishermen convert the world, and why are half a billion Christians unable to repeat the feat?' The answer he gives to his question is: 'The Spirit makes the difference.'[1]

The same writer goes on to tell a story that captures something of the difference between a Spirit-filled faith and one that lacks the Spirit. A poor family was emigrating, taking the boat to America. The parents had barely scraped together the money for the boat, and they had brought along as much bread and cheese as they could carry. After three days of bread and cheese, one of the children told his father that he couldn't stand cheese sandwiches, and that he felt like he would die if he ate any more. The father took pity on him, gave him a small coin from their savings, and sent him off to the ship's galley to buy himself an ice cream. Some time later, the boy came back smiling from ear to ear. When his father asked what he'd been up to, he told him: 'I've had three ice creams, and a dinner. There's no charge

---

1. Peter Kreeft, *Fundamentals of the Faith: Essays in Christian Apologetics* (San Francisco: Ignatius Press, 1988), p. 142.

for the food; it is included in the ticket price. And by the way, here's your coin back.'

The food analogy is very apt: when it comes to faith, many Christians make do with a diet that barely suffices. While they may not be malnourished, there can be a lingering under-nourishment. But we do not have to limp along in the practice of our faith, and quitting is not the only alternative. There is more on offer than we may have been led to believe.

Let me stress that this is not about pouring cold water on those who are hanging on by their fingertips, or those who have a rueful sense that in the practice of their faith they are doing little more than going through the motions. Anyone who feels this way is in the company of some of the greatest saints. The point is that we might recognise that there is more on offer: our faith holds out greater blessings than we have yet received. Jesus himself compares the life of faith to a precious pearl or a buried treasure. It is the Spirit who convinces us of this. It is in the Spirit that we come to realise that every effort we make to live the life of faith will be answered with 'a good measure, pressed down, shaken together, running over' (Lk 6:38).

'The Spirit makes the difference.' God's Holy Spirit is, as the Creed tells us, 'the Lord, the giver of life'. We owe all life to the Spirit. We respect and protect human life, from conception to natural ending, because as a gift of God it is not a commodity, but something priceless. It is the Spirit who puts the priceless gift of life into our faith, a faith which otherwise remains a stale commodity.

If there is to be faith in our life, there needs to be life in our faith; if our faith is lifeless, then we are more at risk of a life that is faithless. For many reasons and in many ways, faith is more problematic today than it was a generation ago. Scandals have done great damage to the life of faith; we have changed from being a society in which belief was valued, to a society in which belief is tolerated; our means of communication and entertainment, far from encouraging faith, routinely call it into question.

The upshot of all this is that even for those who practise their faith, there can be a certain timidity, even a degree of embarrassment. Difficulties like those I have mentioned can sap the life from our faith – and the faith from our life. But the good news is that we are not the first generation to experience such challenges. One of the prophets in the Old Testament tells us how, at a certain point, the people of God complained: 'Our bones are dried up, and our hope is lost.' God's answer to his people's dryness and distress was: 'I will put my Spirit within you, and you shall live' (Ez 37:11, 14).

If our faith is not as life-filled as it might be, it may help to recall that in the history of our religion it has been common for people to feel that their faith has become dry and lifeless. God's answer to this has always been the gift of his Spirit. The Spirit is 'the Lord, the giver of life'.

The faith equivalent of cheese sandwiches may keep us on our feet, but there is so much more on offer, and the Lord, the giver of life, wants us to have it. Let us ask for this gift; let us pray to the Third Person of the Trinity, God's Holy Spirit:

Come, Holy Spirit, fill the hearts of your faithful,
and kindle in them the fire of your love;
send forth your Spirit and they shall be created,
and you shall renew the face of the earth.

Who Proceeds from the Father and the Son

What are we like when we are in love? How do we feel when the people we care most about are healthy, honourable and prospering? Is there a particular shape to our lives when we are looking forward to being reunited with a loved one whom we haven't seen for some time? What happens to us when we are experiencing beauty or delight? In answer to such questions, wouldn't it be true to say that in all these circumstances, one thing we are *not*, is wrapped up in ourselves? Love and beauty and joy draw us out of ourselves; to be in love, or to behold beauty, or to experience joy, is to be outside of oneself.

Think of the most loving person you know. What is she or he like? Always there for others? A constant readiness to give, to be present? Lives a life that looks a bit like an ongoing procession in the direction of other people? In everyday language, it might seem a slightly stilted expression, but when people are anchored in love, beauty and happiness, they are 'proceeding out of themselves'. This is what the Creed tells us about the Holy Spirit: the Spirit 'proceeds from the Father and the Son'. The Spirit is the eternal love and beauty and joy of God.

At this point, our imagination can fail us, because we are used to thinking of love and joy as things that people experience, rather than as a person. But the truth our faith puts before us is that in the life of God, the love between Father and Son is so complete, so total as to be a person: the Third Person of the Trinity, the Holy Spirit. Sometimes the facts of theology really are very close to the facts of life: we don't need a theologian to tell us that the love between two human beings can lead to the creation of a third person. And if the Bible tells us that we are made in the image and likeness of God, we see a particular reflection of that image in the way in which people continue to be made.

The earliest theologians of the Church saw the Spirit's proceeding from the Father and the Son as a kind of explosion of joy; they were mindful that joy is the very heart of God. This might prompt us to ask ourselves if joy is anywhere close to the heart of our faith; perhaps a good question to ask, given the common propensity to see faith and faithfulness as a kind of drudgery.

The Holy Spirit proceeds from the Father and the Son, as the expression of their joy. But if joy is at the heart of God and the heart of our faith, this must give rise to some questions. First, if our faith is all about joy, we might wonder why faith is so widely ignored, despised, rejected and resisted? The answer is actually quite simple: faith invites us to real joy, but in doing so, it calls us to put away false joys. No man on earth can be a faithful husband and a philanderer. If he is to be a true lover of his wife, he must ruthlessly kill any desire for the false little joy that infidelity might offer.

Likewise, our faith calls us to bypass cul-de-sacs, to kill off false joys, so that we can be true, authentic human beings, able to possess lasting joy instead of being possessed by desires for joys that do not last. So yes, our faith is killjoy! When voices in our secular culture make this criticism, they probably do not realise just how accurate they are. But what they miss is that this killjoy faith of ours is nothing other than an invitation to joy. The most vigorous plants are the ones that have been well and wisely pruned, and if we never consent to some pruning, then whatever little joy we find may turn out to be a highway to chaos and misery.

A second question: if joy is at the heart of our faith, what does this say to a world in which there is a great deal of sorrow? Christians are not called to deny suffering, or to brush it away with an easy appeal to God's goodness. If joy is at the heart of our faith, then our task as Christ's faithful is to seek to bring authentic joy into this aching world. Our task is to hold our faith – or better, to let our faith hold us – in such a way that we do not despair when life brings suffering. Mature Christians are wonderful models for us, not just for what they *do*, but also for what they *don't*: they don't lapse into despair, even when life is at its most testing. In seeking to be that kind of Christian, we become better able to bear some of this world's burdens, better able to support those who are vulnerable.

A final question – this time, a slightly odd-sounding one. Is it possible to remember the future? Yes, it is. We know that it is possible to forget the future: when a person slips into despair, they are beginning to forget that they have a future. The consequences can be tragic. Our faith invites us to remember that the future is in God's hands; to remember this is not to be spared suffering, but to have a shield against despair. If we remember that joy – the joy that is at the heart of God and of our faith – remains a possibility

113

for ourselves and our world, then we are better placed to strive for it, rather than becoming consumed by whatever sadness life will inevitably bring. 'We know that all things work together for good for those who love God, who are called according to his purpose' (Rm 8:28).

Who with the Father and the Son is Adored and Glorified

It was once remarked of a certain successful businessman: 'He's a self-made man and he adores his maker.' What does it mean to 'adore' someone? There is something instantly off-putting about the idea of someone adoring themselves. At the very least, it sounds comical, and on a more serious note, we would not expect the man who adores himself to make a very good husband. Even if we have not a ready definition for adoration, we know instinctively that self-adoration would be no adoration.

Adoration can be used as a figure of speech, and in common usage we may speak about someone adoring chocolate, or wine, or a fillet steak! But when we speak about adoring in the proper, religious sense, in the sense in which the Holy Spirit, along with the Father and the Son, is adored and glorified, we are talking about something quite different. When we say that we adore God, this means something more than fondness – although it is, of course, a great blessing to feel fondness for the person of Jesus. When we say we adore God, Father, Son and Spirit, we are saying something about our deepest, innermost selves. Adoration is an attitude that comes from the very deepest part of who we are.

It would be a desperate misunderstanding to imagine that to adore God is to put ourselves down. When we get down on our knees, in a posture and attitude of adoration and praise of God, we are actually raising ourselves up, in our dignity as the beloved children of God. When we adore, we are in touch with our deepest selves.

An intriguing thing about adoration, whether it is adoration of the Lord's presence in the Blessed Sacrament or a prayerful attitude in some other context, is that it is utterly impractical. Adoration is not a *means* to an end – it *is* an end. When we adore God, we are being what we are made to be, doing what we have been created to do.

Does this still sound a bit like self-abasement? Does it leave a lingering suspicion that the reason for our existence is to put ourselves down by bowing down? If so, then consider how you feel when you witness beauty. Does a gorgeous sunset make you feel like a lesser human being, because you are standing in awe at its beauty? Are you diminished by your admiration of it? Do you feel the need to hold back, and not overdo your admiration in case it takes from your dignity? Of course not. Your admiration is a gift; it enhances your human dignity. Things that are truly praiseworthy call forth our human dignity – they don't overturn it. And adoration is the highest form of praise – indeed, it is something beyond praise, reserved for the one who is beyond every created thing.

Another liberating thing about this profound attitude that we call adoration is that it does not depend on our circumstances or on our feelings. For various reasons, at any given time I may not feel joyful before the Lord; I may not feel thankful; I may not feel praise of God arising within me. But in all my circumstances, I can get down on my knees and let God be God – or stand up, for that matter, and spread out my hands and without the need for thoughts or words, let God be God. In doing that, I am not only praying deeply, I am asserting a little bit of freedom, irrespective of my circumstances.

We might think of the striking words of Etty Hillesum, which she wrote while in a detainment camp in the Netherlands, before being shipped to Auschwitz by the Nazi authorities: 'There will always be a small patch of sky above, and there will always be enough space to fold two hands in prayer.'[1] What a powerful expression of a freedom that no law and no tyrant can ever touch. What a sad pity if we should ever reject or devalue that freedom!

The Creed states that the Holy Spirit, along with the Father and the Son, is *adored and glorified*. How do we glorify God? Simply by seeking to live a life that reflects something of his goodness. It is our innermost, deepest self that adores; it is only good sense that our practical self, our decision-making, our day-to-day living, should follow suit. When this happens, we give glory to the one whom we adore.

For Christians, the Spirit is not some vague force, enabling us to boast about being 'spiritual', while living a life that does not give the Holy Spirit a look-in. God's Holy Spirit, whom we adore, is our magnetic north, our guide, our enabler. There is nothing vague or wooly about living an authentic Christian life: to do so is, as St Paul puts it, to

---

1. Etty Hillesum, *An Interrupted Life*, p. 221.

'walk by the Spirit' (Gal 5:16). May our efforts to live that life lead us to adore God, and may our adoration help us in those same efforts.

Who Has Spoken Through the Prophets

The Creed tells us that the Holy Spirit is a person who has spoken. Our God is a God who communicates. At the very beginning of the Bible, we read how God spoke reality into existence: 'God said, "let there be light", and there was light' (Gn 1:3). Jesus is described as the 'Word' of God: 'The Word became flesh and dwelt among us' (Jn 1:14). Our God is not a silent God, but a God who has things to say to us – things to guide, to correct, to heal, to console, to give hope.

It might be a little easier if God were silent – or at least if he didn't speak words that challenge, but when God speaks, he does so in order to comfort the afflicted and to afflict the comfortable. And it is the Spirit of God who speaks through the prophets. The most important and influential prophets are the prophets of the Bible, but the voice of prophecy continues in the Church and in the world.

When people seek to live a Spirit-filled life, a life open to God, they very often become mouthpieces for God. If we were to name a couple of modern prophets, we might think of someone like Blessed Teresa of Calcutta, whose own work with the poorest of the poor led her to see that the teaching of Christ can be virtually summed up in just five words that can be taught on a person's fingers, in the manner in which one might teach a small child to count. Blessed Theresa would sometimes take a person's hand, and repeat the words of Jesus on their fingers: 'You did it to me' (Mt 25:40). We might also think of Pope Francis, who has reminded us that 'the proclamation of the saving love of God comes before moral and religious imperatives'.[1] In other words, the starting point of our Christian faith is what God has done for us, not anything we have done for God; and our efforts to live a life that is moral and just are a *response* to God's love, rather than an attempt to earn it.

What, then, about the biblical prophets? These were people whom God called when believers had become careless in responding to God's love; when people had become unfaithful in their relationship with the Lord. God then called prophets to remind his people of how to live and pray and act. These prophets often had a two-sided message: they spoke stern words of correction and they spoke consoling words of hope. They reminded people that their sinfulness would lead them to misery but that God's love would heal and restore them.

The trouble was – and still is – that people do not like to be corrected. God asked the prophets to speak, but the people told them to be quiet (cf. Am 2:12). Then, as now, there was a temptation only to want the sugar coating and not the pill. That temptation was behind what the people once said to the prophet Isaiah: 'Do not be telling us what is right; speak to us smooth things, prophesy illusions … let us hear no more of the Holy One of Israel' (cf. Is 30:10-11). But God loved his people too much to leave them uncorrected

1. Pope Francis interviewed by Antonio Spadaro SJ, 'A Big Heart Open to God', *America: The National Catholic Review* (30 September 2013).

when they strayed; in this, God was like a father correcting a child.

The word of God is critical of a prophecy that is timid or falsely optimistic. On one occasion, God complained about false prophets through the prophet Jeremiah: 'They have healed the wound of my people too lightly, saying "peace, peace", when there is no peace' (Jer 6:15). That is a powerful expression: 'they have healed people's wounds too lightly.' If my life is a mess, the last thing I need is for someone to say 'You're just fine'. This will not help me at all – in fact, if I believe it, it will stop me from getting better. Sometimes upsetting news from the doctor is what saves a patient's life. Sometimes upsetting news from the prophets is what calls us to a better life.

Here is a smattering of thoughts from the prophets of the Old Testament. Through the prophet Isaiah, God tells the people that he cannot stand their worship, that he does not want their prayers and sacrifices, unless they are also making an honest attempt to live a life of kindness and compassion towards others: 'I cannot stand assemblies with iniquity' (Is 1:13); 'Though you pray at length, I will not listen; your hands are stained with crime' (Is 1:15). A lovely line in the prophet Hosea conveys God's dream for us: he wants us to be wise, to live well, to be happy. This is why he complains: 'My people are destroyed for lack of knowledge' (Hos 4:6). God does not want to leave us in the dark: he wants us to know what is good and right and just, and to live by that knowledge.

The biblical prophets also promised God's favour, a time of renewal. Through the prophet Ezekiel, God made this promise to his people: 'I will give you a new heart, and put a new spirit in you. I will take out of your flesh the heart of stone and give you a heart of flesh' (Ez 36:26). On another occasion, the prophet Joel spoke these words on God's behalf: 'I will restore to you the years the swarming locust has eaten' (Jl 2:25). I once heard a priest who had lost years of his life to alcoholism describe what hope he took from those words. God's Spirit, speaking through the biblical prophets, can touch the spirits of broken people – and of a broken world – today.

Finally, the Spirit can speak with the voice of prophecy in our own conscience. What is the biggest obstacle to God in my life? If I can answer this, I am being open to the Spirit's prophetic voice. Equally I could ask: What am I most cynical about? Where do we most need hope? It is in the spaces hollowed out by such questions that the prophetic voice of God's Holy Spirit can speak to us today.

I Believe in One

If you want to check whether an item of gold or silver is authentic, you will look for the hallmark. Once you have found that discrete mark, you will be reassured that you are not dealing with a bit of cheap metal posing as the real thing. From early times, Christians spoke about certain hallmarks that indicated the genuineness of the Church. There were four such hallmarks, and for centuries they have been referred to simply as the 'marks of the Church'. We list them in the Creed when we say: 'I believe in *one, holy, catholic* and *apostolic* Church.'

These words are signed up to not only by Roman Catholics, but by Christians of various traditions. As a part of our ancient Creed, these marks date back to before most of the divisions in the Church, which means that virtually all Christians have a sense of ownership of them. Granted, these marks are not understood in the same way by all Christians; the words 'one' and 'catholic,' for example, can mean somewhat different things to a Roman Catholic and an Anglican.

First, though, let us consider the question: Why have a Church at all? To which we might add: Why have any organised religion? Why not let each person make their own way to God? The simple answer is that this is not what

God wanted. The Lord has a tailor-made call and plan for each of us, but he does not call us in isolation, and he does not call us to live in isolation. The Bible tells us that Christ is the head of a body (cf. Col 1:18), not of a vast number of isolated individuals; together, the disciples of Christ make up a body.

This means that if any of us ever wants to assess our discipleship, some of the first questions we should ask are: How do I treat others? What is my attitude to those around me? It also means that we must dismiss the idea that we can find our own way to God, in splendid isolation, and with contempt for organised religion.

But when we consider some of the failings of organised religion, might we not wonder if the world would be a better place if it, along with the Church, were abolished altogether? There is a fairly straightforward answer to this objection too. Without in any way downplaying the sins and crimes that have been perpetrated by 'religious' people, we would be very naïve to think that such things would disappear if an institution were abolished. Sin of every kind lies deep in every human heart. As the Lord once said to Cain: 'Sin is lurking at your door; its desire is for you; you must master it' (Gn 4:7).

The Church is nothing other than the people called by God, as disciples of Christ, in the life and power of the Holy Spirit. Despite all the brokenness and division of history, Christians keep saying that they believe in *one* church. Our various traditions want us to do this, and when Catholics and Christians of other traditions stand in their respective congregations on Sunday morning and profess our belief that the church is *one*, we are engaging in a wonderful act of trust in God; we are expressing the hope and trust that the oneness for which Christ prayed will come to pass, despite our divisions.

Christ prayed for that oneness shortly before he died. 'Father,' he said, 'may they all be one, as you and I are one' (Jn 17:21). If our oneness was Christ's dying wish, then we need to take it seriously. We need, at the very least, to avoid anything that gives rise to division – and not only division between churches; also, division between Christians. What does sin bring about? What is the first effect of selfishness? Division! When people offend each other, they fall out; those who were once friends find that their relationship has fallen apart. What does love do? It unites! Saint Paul writes that it is love that binds everything together in perfect harmony (cf. Col 3:14).

God's plan – God's desire – for the relationship between different churches and traditions is exactly the same as his plan for the relationship between individuals: it is a plan of unity and reconciliation; it is a plan for communion. This begins to come about when individual believers and different traditions seek renewal, when each of us tries to draw a little closer to God in our day-to-day living, when we try to pray in earnest, when we strive to live a life marked by goodness, compassion and forgiveness. When we pray the words 'I believe in one church', we would do well to imagine the Lord asking us gently: 'How are you attempting to live as a person of communion?'

Holy

When, as we recite the Creed, we say the words 'I believe in one, holy, Catholic and apostolic Church', the word 'holy' may pose a certain challenge. To the extent that we have some difficulty with the idea that the Church is holy, this can arise for two reasons. First, the idea of holiness is often misunderstood, with the result that it can get some bad press.

'She is terribly holy, but you wouldn't want to get on the wrong side of her.' Many of us have heard some such expression. It is used of a person who prays devoutly, but whose prayer doesn't quite seem to get lived out in Christian virtues such as kindness, patience and charity of speech. But what kind of holiness is it that can talk nicely to God, then turn around and fleece one of God's beloved children? Actually, it is no kind of holiness. It may not be blatant hypocrisy – we are not qualified to judge anyone in that way – but at the very least, that kind of 'holiness' is immature and lopsided. Holiness – genuine holiness – is lovely, attractive, appealing. Genuine holiness is a true and effective advertisement for God and for the life that God wants us to lead. We should remember this if ever we encounter a kind of 'holiness' that is off-putting.

There is a second reason why we might take issue with the idea that the Church is holy: the obvious and undeniable fact that sin, scandal and a lack of compassion have often been found in the Church. In recent years, we have become aware of scandalous failings. Earlier generations sometimes faced a real lack of compassion in the way that the demands of the faith were presented. Some of the older people in our midst may recall a time when the Catholic faith, as preached and practiced in Ireland, was more a matter of compulsion than a matter of compassion.

And yet, we profess to believe that the Church is holy. So just what is holiness? Holiness is two things. First of all, to be holy is to be called by God, to be set apart for a particular task and with a particular identity. This aspect of holiness is pure gift – it has nothing to do with the behaviour of Christians and everything to do with the free choice of God, who has loved the world to the point of offering his Son.

The second part of holiness is to live a life that is in keeping with God's gift and call, a life that is a response to God's goodness. This is the part of holiness that can shine less than brightly when Christians do not live up to their calling. But the first part of holiness remains; it remains in the Church, always. The Church remains loved by God, called by God, set apart for a special purpose, which is to be a light for the world.

Think of parents who dearly love their child. Their love is pure gift – it didn't begin because the child did something very special; it was poured out from day one, before the child could do anything. That child is and remains a beloved son or daughter, irrespective of whether he or she does well or badly. But it is in the nature of love to call forth a response, and if the child grows up to be selfish, ungrateful, unloving, then even if the parents' love remains constant, there is something lacking. When the love shown by the parents does not meet with love in the child, the child may still be loved, but he or she is failing to live as a beloved child.

At times, the Church fails to live as God's beloved child. But from God's side, the love is constant, the call is constant. For this reason, we can say that the Church is holy, because it is God's choice that guarantees real holiness. When we say that despite her failings, the Church is holy, we are saying that God's call has not gone away – it is constant, like the love of parents for a wayward child is constant.

How, then, should we react to the lack of holiness that can be evident in our Church? One reaction is to insist that the Church can no longer speak with a clear, distinctive, authoritative voice, no longer offer a message that is fresh and challenging and hope-filled. But that reaction can become a kind of collective self-harm. If suffering and disappointment lead us to reject the very possibility of goodness, our pain can only increase. We can end up like a starving person refusing to believe there is such a thing as food.

The only sane response to a *lack* of holiness is the *pursuit* of holiness, in the knowledge that God's call to the Church, and to each one of us, is constant. For broken, sinful human beings, the pursuit of holiness has a name, and that name is 'repentance'. On our way to the holiness (the genuine, lovely, attractive holiness to which we are called by God), our roadmap is repentance – a realistic, humble acknowledgment of the sin that is found in the Church as a whole and in each of us. As the *Catechism of the Catholic Church* puts it: 'In everyone, the weeds of sin will still be mixed with the good wheat of the Gospel until the end of time. Hence the Church gathers sinners already caught up in Christ's salvation but still on the way to holiness.'[1]

That's us, that's the Church. Beloved, sinners, pilgrims: holy, yet still on the way to holiness.

---

1. *Catechism of the Catholic Church*, 827.

Catholic

It is only very rarely that the Church excommunicates people, and on some of those rare occasions the Church has been decried as monstrous, cruel and illiberal. It might come as a surprise, then, to hear that occasionally, people have been excommunicated for not being liberal enough!

Back in the middle of the twentieth century, a Jesuit priest named Leonard Feeney, based in Massachusetts, made a name for himself by his firebrand preaching. What brought him to the attention of Church authorities was his insistence that all non-Catholics were on their way to hell. All the prayer and charity in the world were no use, according to Father Feeney: unless a person was a member of the Roman Catholic Church, he or she was damned. End of story. No discussion. In 1953, he was excommunicated for persistently teaching what was contrary to Catholic faith. He was eventually reconciled to the Church, and it is rather ironic that the most important lesson he managed to impart was that if you persistently teach that all those outside the Church are damned, then you will find yourself outside the Church.

Father Feeney actually took his lead from a third-century bishop, St Cyprian, who coined the phrase, 'Outside the Church, there is no salvation'. This phrase is official Catholic teaching; so what was the problem with what Fr Feeney had taught? When the Church states that there is no salvation outside the Church, it is *not* saying that if your name isn't in a Roman Catholic baptismal register you are damned. Rather, it is expressing the conviction that God has given the Church everything that is needed for the permanent and final good of men and women – a good which we call 'salvation'.

This does not mean that none of this goodness is found elsewhere; what is at issue here is the faith conviction that the Church has been, and remains, gifted with all that God is offering to his children. Does the Church always live up to the blessings it has received? Obviously not. Are individual Catholics necessarily better than individual members of other faiths and traditions? Obviously not. In fact, if we give the matter some thought, the claim to have received all the blessings God is offering should humble us, because it is a claim we most certainly do not live up to.

The word 'catholic' means universal. It is another irony, then, that for some members of the Church, 'Catholic' is little more than a badge of identity, a badge that tells the world who we are not: not Protestant, not Jewish, not Buddhist. But this is a terrible impoverishment, because the Catholic Church, if it lives up to its name, is meant to be universal. It is called to embrace the whole world with the wisdom and goodness of God.

A congregation at Mass, whether in a small country church or in the cathedral of a great city, is connected to the whole world. The nature of this connection is charity, the love of God. Our Catholic faith should make our spirits grow rather than shrink; it should give us a heart that is open to others, that desires to share the love of God with others. Do we sense that our Catholic faith does this? If we have no such sense, then we must acknowledge that the best is yet to come.

Perhaps we can see something of that universality in our recent popes. Saint John Paul II wanted to embrace the world with the love of Christ – and he travelled constantly as a sign of that embrace. Benedict XVI wanted the world to understand the love of Christ – and he taught and wrote about the Lord with a unique clarity. Pope Francis wants the world to live out of that embrace and by that knowledge, and he is teaching the universal faith with a wonderful, urgent simplicity.

The *Catechism of the Catholic Church* tells us the Church is catholic, or universal, in two senses.[1] First, in the sense that it has been blessed with all that the Lord offers. As I have suggested, this should never be a cause of boasting, only a cause of gratitude, and perhaps even of a certain humiliation when we realise how poorly we respond to God's goodness. The second sense in which the Church is catholic, or universal, is that she is sent by Christ to proclaim the Good News of salvation to all of humanity. In a nutshell, the fact that the Church is catholic means that we have a treasure and a task: the treasure is the faith we have been given; the task is to live that faith in such a way that we share it and spread it.

This is simply the pattern of life: if you are a talented athlete, athletics is your treasure, and also your task; if you are a budding musician, then music is both your treasure and your task. Even more so, if you have children, they are your treasure and your task. Our Catholic faith is not

---

1. *Catechism of the Catholic Church*, 830–1.

a badge of exclusiveness: it is a blessing, a treasure. Do we treasure it? It is not a personal possession, but something to be lived in a way that is a blessing for others. Are we ready for that task?

And Apostolic Church

In recent years, food traceability has become a big issue. We now expect to be able to trace everything we eat, right back to where it was produced. Traceability 'from farm to fork' has become an advertising boast for many food producers.

While food traceability is relatively recent, 'faith traceability' is as old as the Church. We can trace our faith right back to the person of Jesus; an unbroken chain of people links us with what the Lord did and said, as he walked the roads of Galilee and Jerusalem.

One of the things that pilgrims to the Holy Land most appreciate is the sense of connection with Jesus. If you visit Galilee, you can take a boat trip on the sea of Galilee; or from many parts of Jerusalem, you can see down into the Kidron Valley, which Jesus regularly crossed on his trips between Jerusalem and Bethany. To be there, to see the sights that Jesus saw, to travel the roads that Jesus travelled, can give a wonderful sense of the concreteness of this person whom we worship as our God and love as our saviour.

Our Christian faith is not built on abstract principles – it is built on a concrete, historical connection with Jesus himself. Anything we have heard and learned about Jesus, we have heard from someone else, and they in turn heard it from someone else. All those 'someone elses' form a chain that reaches right back to Jesus.

Jesus was not widely travelled. He did not address large assemblies or congregations. He called a small group of people, and he had two purposes in mind when he called them: first, they were to be with him; second, they were to be sent out to preach his message (cf. Mk 3:14). The word 'apostle' means 'one who is sent'. The apostles were the first link in the chain that connects us with the historical, flesh-and-blood person of Jesus.

We could ask ourselves, 'For me, who has been the most recent link in that chain? From whom did I receive my faith?' Parents, in the majority of cases, sow the seed of faith. It can be strengthened by teachers, priests, friends and workmates. However each of us might describe the most recent link in this chain, it is a chain that goes right back to the apostles, those who walked with Jesus, and witnessed his words and deeds.

When we stand and say the Lord's Prayer together, we are reciting words that Jesus taught his earliest followers. On one occasion, the Lord said to his followers: 'When you pray, pray like this ...' Then he taught them to say, 'Our Father ...' This prayer has been passed on to us by an unbroken chain of people who have prayed it themselves. Our faith, then, is *traceable* – we can trace it right back to the person of Jesus.

When we say, in the Creed, that we 'believe in one, holy, catholic and apostolic Church' we are expressing this confidence in traceability: we know our origins; we are sure that what we believe is the genuine article.

The Church is apostolic in three ways.[1] First of all, because it is built on the foundation of the apostles (cf. Eph 2:20). These earliest witnesses, chosen and sent out on mission by the Lord himself, passed on what they had seen and heard. They are our earliest historical link with Jesus. Second, the Church is apostolic in the sense that it preserves and passes on the teachings of the apostles. Before his passion, Jesus told the apostles that the Holy Spirit would 'guide them into all the truth' (Jn 16:13). As time passed, with prayer and reflection, the Church's understanding of the faith grew and deepened. This growth and deepening are the fulfilment of that promise of Jesus, that the Spirit would lead his followers to a deeper understanding.

The Church uses a lovely term to describe the teaching which is passed on from one generation to another: 'the deposit of faith'. Faith is not a set of abstractions; it is about a life that is lived out in a concrete way. But that life is based on a body of clear teachings and principles. Unlike a deposit in a bank, the deposit of faith does not decrease when we draw on it: instead, the more we draw on it, the more we use it to give shape to our lives, the greater the 'deposit' gets. We could reflect on this, and ask ourselves if we actually draw on this deposit, rather than subscribing to it like some fine theory that we keep safe and undisturbed in a vault in our minds.

The third sense in which the Church is apostolic is that she has been guided and taught by an unbroken chain of successors to the apostles. These successors are the bishops, whose main responsibility is not administration, but the teaching of the faith. Have you ever been struck by the fact

---

1. Cf. *Catechism of the Catholic Church*, 857.

that in every Mass we pray for the local bishop by name? This is a recognition of the fact that his task is both difficult and important, and so he needs our prayers. We do well to recall this, in a time when all authority figures, not least bishops, are subject to cynicism and criticism.

We are blessed to be able to trace our faith; we can be confident that it is the genuine article, that it is what Christ wanted to give to us. But let us be sure that we also live by it, in the way that Christ wants us to live.

I Confess One Baptism for the Forgiveness of Sins

In the Catholic faith, colour is very important. Two colours are often associated with the beginning and the end of life, almost like bookends. When an infant is brought for Baptism, at a certain point in the ceremony he or she is wrapped in a white garment, while the priest says the words: 'You have become a new creation, and clothed yourself in Christ. See in this white garment the outward sign of your Christian dignity. With your family and friends to help you by word and example, bring that dignity unstained into the everlasting life of heaven.'

Later, when the time comes for the believer to leave this life, purple is the dominant colour. Many people imagine that because purple figures prominently at funerals, it is the colour of mourning. But the original reason purple was used at funerals is that it was the colour of wealth. In biblical times, it took great skill and expense to produce purple dye, and only the wealthiest could afford purple robes. The purple we see at funerals is a sign of God's great wealth – a wealth that far outdoes our human poverty, a poverty we sense most acutely in illness, tragedy and death.

We could mention other colours – green and red, rose and gold. In addition to colour, there are other things that make the practice of our faith very concrete, tangible, physical. In our worship, we use everyday things like bread and water; we use wine and oil and flame and light and touch. These are the raw material of our sacraments, and they can remind us of two things. First, since God has created us as flesh and blood, as physical creatures, we approach God in a physical way. Second, God approaches us in the same way – through ordinary, everyday things. This is the essence of our sacraments: they are rituals and actions in which we encounter God, and God comes to us, by means of physical things.

We have seven sacraments, but Baptism is the only one mentioned in the Creed. The Creed cannot possibly cover all the territory of our Christian living and worship: it covers the fundamentals, and Baptism is the fundamental sacrament. Baptism is given only once (this is why we say that we confess 'one Baptism'), and it is through Baptism that we are introduced into the life of faith. The other sacraments are given only to those who are already baptised.

The Creed states that Baptism is 'for the forgiveness of sins'. We can understand this better if we recall that Baptism was originally administered to adults, who were aware of their sinfulness and their need of God's grace and mercy. These people had prepared for years; they yearned for the day of their Baptism; they longed to 'walk in newness of life' (Rm 6:4). They knew, when they were being plunged into the waters of Baptism, that they were being cleansed of all sin; they knew that they were beginning a new life of discipleship.

Later, when it became common practice to baptise infants, the understanding was that the adults who were presenting the children for Baptism were taking on the responsibility of introducing the little ones to the life of grace, the life of discipleship. It was up to the adults to create the kind of families and communities where God would be found. In that sense, it could still be said that the infant was being removed from a world of sinfulness and brought into the life of Christ. Obviously an infant has not committed any sins, but in Baptism the child is brought into the life of Christ, in whom is all forgiveness.

Do you remember the story, in the Old Testament, of Moses leading the Chosen People out of slavery in Egypt, through the waters of the Red Sea, on their way to freedom in the Promised Land? The earliest Christians understood Baptism in the light of that story: it was through the waters of Baptism, rather than the waters of the Red Sea, that they passed on their way to freedom. It was from slavery to sin, meaninglessness, despair and death, rather than from slavery in Egypt, that they were being set free. Their Promised Land was not a location but a life: the new life in Christ, which began with Baptism and would be completed in the next world.

That was how our forebears understood things; that is our inheritance. Baptism is the introduction to a way of life. But if Baptism is about a way of life, then it must be lived. What does it mean to live our Baptism?

Baptism introduces us into the life of Christ, but it does not remove us from the struggles that are part and parcel of our human life. We are sinners; we will always be prone to taking the wrong turn, to slipping backwards, to getting wrapped up in ourselves, to losing our way. For this reason, the Christian life is a life of combat, a life of struggle. And this is why St Paul, the earliest theologian of Baptism, could say that to be baptised is to die with Christ (cf. Rm 6:1-11). To be plunged into the waters of Baptism was to drown the sinner, so that the saint could come to life.

This is the drama of Christian discipleship: allowing what is sinful to be put to death, so that we can truly walk in newness of life. This does not happen all at once; it is a lifelong affair. Our walking can be more about baby steps than confident strides, but it is by persevering in those faltering steps and picking ourselves up whenever we fall that we live out our Baptism, that we live the life which Christ has opened up for us.

And I Look Forward to the Resurrection of the Dead

One thing we all have in common, irrespective of age, occupation, health or any other factor, is death: we will all die – each and every one of us, without exception. There are those who say that it is morbid to dwell on this, but commonsense should tell us that it is morbid to deny the inevitable. 'How would you live, if you had only a certain amount of time left?' That is not a helpful question, because it contains the misleading little word, 'if'. When it comes to death, there is no 'if'. There is only 'when'. A far better question would be, 'How am I making the best of the time – the limited time – that is granted to me?'

Have you noticed how reluctant many people have become even to use the word 'death'? More and more, we hear the expression 'passed on' or even simply 'passed'. Ironically, even as it seeks to avoid the reality of death, this kind of language points to the Christian understanding of death. Death is, in fact, a 'passing on', a passage into a new life. Faithful Christians, and all those who have sought to live a life of integrity, can anticipate God's welcome into that life.

If you were to do a poll of your friends and workmates, asking them what they thought happened to people once they died, you can be sure that you would get a broad spectrum of answers. Christians who are confident in their faith will be able to tell you what they believe, but from others you will also hear it said that once we die, that's it. Nothingness. It is over. Some will tell you that when we die, we go back to the stars, we blend back into the elements from which we came. And some people will tell you that they believe in reincarnation: when we die, we come back again for another shot at life. To these guesses, our Christian faith responds with clarity: we are not destined for nothingness; we are not stardust on our way back to the stars from which we came; and we do not get recycled. We have a destiny and a destination. This life is not a dress rehearsal, but a time-limited journey, a pilgrimage.

At the beginning of the Creed, we state our conviction that God has made all things, including ourselves. We did not come about by some fluke, but were willed into existence by a loving Father. Now, near the end of the Creed, we state the conviction that this existence of ours is not destined to be snuffed out, but changed. As one of the prayers of the funeral Mass says: 'For your faithful, Lord, life is changed not ended.' Or as St Thérèse of Lisieux said on her deathbed: 'I am not dying; I am entering life.'

But just what is resurrection? At the very beginning of the Christian religion, St Paul took to task some people who were asking what might, to our ears, sound like reasonable questions: 'How are the dead raised? What kind of body will they have?' (1 Cor 15:35). But St Paul said that questions are foolish because they miss the point – the point being that the life to come simply can't be described in the limited terms of this present life.

That said, however, the word 'resurrection' itself is a lovely – and interesting – word. When we meet someone who has been ill, we might say to them, 'It's good to see you back on your feet'. In St Paul's language, that's just what resurrection conveys: the idea that we're put back on our feet, but in a way that we can't quite describe or conceptualise. It is often the case that we are unable to picture the promise; to see, or imagine, what our faith holds out to us. Happily, the limitation is in us, rather than in the reality itself. But even a partial image can give us hope: our loved ones who have died are destined to be put back on their feet! And that is our destiny too: life, real life, up-and-about life.

There is no denying the reality of death: it is very real indeed and the signs of it are all about us. We encounter illness, infirmity, uncertainty, the death of our loved ones; but we are not crushed by those signs, because we have hope. This hope is not mathematical knowledge, yet it is a valid way of looking at reality. Our Christian hope interprets the desire we have for life. It tells us that this desire is not an evolutionary blip, but a pointer to reality.

What's more, our hope has a name: Jesus Christ. The one who 'was crucified under Pontius Pilate, suffered death and was buried' is the one who 'rose again on the third day'. Our whole religion, our prayer, our devotion, our Mass, is centred on a person who was once dead, but now lives. It is in him, in Jesus Christ, that our faith in the resurrection of the dead is anchored.

The resurrection of Christ, and the resurrection of the dead, are the focus of Christian hope – a hope which is not only for this life (cf. 1 Cor 15:19). We do not work out our hopes, or reduce them to neat theories. We take hold of them and seek to let them take hold of us, so that we might live by them. Let us do the same with the hope of eternal life, which we hold out for ourselves and for our departed loved ones.

And the Life of the World to Come

When we say, as we recite the Creed, that we 'look forward' to the next life, this does not mean that we are gleefully anticipating the end of our life in this world. The words 'I look forward to' translate the Latin word *exspecto*, which means 'I expect'. We experience death as an unwelcome intruder, and the Creed is not asking us to paper over this hard fact. Rather, the Creed teaches us to *expect* that death will be followed by life. Death is not the end – we fully anticipate that it will give way to new life.

It has been observed that there are two kinds of person who are fearless in the face of death. One is the indomitable pagan warrior whose only fear is to lose honour and appear cowardly. The other is the Christian martyr who goes fearlessly to the place of execution. The pagan warrior is fearless because he has no regard for his life; the martyr loves life, but is fearless because he has no regard for death.

There is a fine, stirring prayer, which priests sometimes speak over the dying, that sounds almost like the sending of a warrior into battle. It captures the courage and trust that can arise from our conviction that death is not the end, but the entry into new life:

Go forth, Christian soul, from this world
in the name of God the almighty Father,
who created you,
in the name of Jesus Christ, the Son of the living God,
who suffered for you,
in the name of the Holy Spirit,
who was poured out upon you.
Go forth, faithful Christian![1]

When that time comes, the destination to which we go forth is what the Creed refers to as 'the life of the world to come'. Let us ponder three questions: What is that life like? What about hell? Is talk of a future life not a distraction from the important business of living in this world?

What is heaven like? We do not know the geography of heaven, but one thing we can say is that those images of bored angels plucking harps while seated on fluffy clouds are nonsense. What the Church's teaching makes clear is that heaven is being in God's presence, and being fully oneself. Heaven is not just a *place* of peace: it is *inner* peace. It is not just coming home: it is coming home to oneself.[2]

Whenever we attempt to describe the indescribable, we use images of various kinds. Among the images the Bible uses for heaven are peace, light, a wedding reception, the house of the Father, a wonderfully beautiful city. On the other hand, St Paul tells us: 'no eye has seen, nor ear heard, nor the human heart conceived, what God has prepared for those who love him' (1 Cor 2:9). When all is said and done, we will just have to wait and see.

---

1. *Catechism of the Catholic Church*, 1020.
2. Ibid., 1025.

What about hell? Eternal life with God is not earned – it is a gift. But it is a gift that must be *chosen*. The constant teaching of Jesus and of the Church is that there is an alternative to heaven. Heaven is our proper destination, but not our inevitable one. If it is not helpful to picture heaven as a place of harp-wielding angels on fluffy clouds, neither is it helpful to picture hell as a place of fork-wielding demons beside roaring furnaces. Hell, quite simply, is separation from God. It is the permanent end of the very possibility of happiness. And it is the infinitely frustrating knowledge that things could have been completely different. Jesus describes this state of sorrow and anger as 'weeping and gnashing of teeth' (Lk 13:28).

The Church's clear teaching on the reality of hell is not a threat; it is a call to responsibility and conversion.[3] It is up to us to use our freedom well, and to repent when we fail to do so. If a parent failed to warn a small child about the dangers of traffic on the road, because they didn't want their child to be afraid of anything, we would rightly say that that parent was neglectful and foolish. Likewise, it would be neglectful and foolish to fail to recognise that our human freedom demands to be well used. This life we've been given is not a dress rehearsal. Let us live it well!

Finally, when Christians look forward to the life of the world to come, are we not indulging in escapism? Does the anticipation of a perfect existence not risk making us neglectful of our responsibilities in this life? Not at all, because the task of Christian living is not just getting people into heaven – it is also a matter of getting heaven into people. We are, after all, the people who pray: 'Thy

---

3. Ibid., 1036.

kingdom come, thy will be done on earth.' Yes, our faith invites us to look forward to a destination, but in the meantime, it urges us to make this world more and more like that destination.

Picture two roads. One is leading nowhere. The other is leading to an important city. Which road will be better maintained?[4] History has shown repeatedly that when there is a decline in the belief that life in this world has a destination, there is often a decline in the care shown for this life and in the commitment shown to this world. Where, for example, do we currently find the greatest concern for end-of-life care? In quarters where belief in eternal life is strongest.

As sinful human beings, we may occasionally lose our way in this life. But we need never lose our address. We have a home, a destination. Even as we commit ourselves to the tasks this life presents to us, we look forward to 'the life of the world to come'.

4. For this image, cf. Peter Kreeft, *Fundamentals of the Faith*, p. 161.

Amen

We are now at the end of the Creed, at the very last word. Every time we recite the Creed, we begin with 'I believe' and we end with 'Amen'. In contemporary terms, the word 'amen' is rather like the signature we write, or, if we are working online, the box we click, in order to show that we accept the terms and conditions that have been outlined to us. Indeed, one and a half millennia ago, St Augustine said: 'He who says *amen* writes his signature.'

The word 'amen' is our signature: it shows that we are not merely reciting the words of the Creed, but that we are buying into them. God's 'terms and conditions' are, of course, a lot different to those of a vendor or a service provider. God only gives. He who has 'spoken through the prophets' has no thought of making a profit. To accept his conditions means to accept a love that is unconditional. God's love is, however, a life-changing love, and when we say our 'amen' to it, we consent to have our lives changed – albeit gradually, and perhaps in fits and starts. When we say 'amen' to God's truth, we say 'yes'; we say 'may it be so'.

But what does the little word 'amen' actually mean? It comes from a Hebrew root, which has two distinct but related meanings. One the one hand, it can mean to be trustworthy, reliable, dependable; on the other hand, it can mean to trust, to believe in. When we say 'amen' we're capturing both of those realities: 'God's faithfulness towards us and our trust in him.'[1]

So this wonderful little word says something about God, and something about us. About God, it says: 'He is real, true, dependable.' About us, it says: 'We are happy to find in God our support, our rock, our anchor.' We can go so far as to say that the word 'amen' captures an entire spirituality. To say 'amen' is to express the conviction that God is trustworthy, and it is to live out that conviction by entrusting ourselves to him. In fact, the whole Christian life can be understood as an 'amen': a trusting in God and a living out of that trust. What a marvellous cargo of meaning in such a small word! It is almost a Creed in and of itself.

In the gospels, the word 'amen' figures prominently on the lips of Jesus, but whereas we speak the word to confirm what we have just heard or prayed, Jesus uses it to introduce what he is about to say. He often begins his teaching by saying, 'Amen, I say to you ...' Which of us would dare to speak this way? This manner of speaking is a sign of the unique authority with which the Lord teaches.

Jesus is our authority, and because he stands behind his words, we can stand on them. As Christians, the authority we follow is not fashion or fad, not opinion poll or majority view, but the teaching of Christ himself. We would do well never to take for granted the guidance and the hope we have in the teaching of the Master. The New Testament describes this hope as an 'anchor of the soul' (Heb 6:19). This wonderful image tells us that if we follow Christ, we

1. *Catechism of the Catholic Church*, 1062.

need not drift aimlessly, like an unanchored ship; if we stand for Christ, we need not fall for anything.

Not only does Jesus use the word 'amen' in this unique way, the Bible tells us that he is the Amen. In the last book of the Bible, the book of Revelation, Jesus is described as 'the Amen, the faithful and true witness' (Rv 3:14). And St Paul tells us: 'Through him, all the promises of God have their "yes", and so we say "amen" through him, to the praise of God' (2 Cor 1:20). Once again, we're being told that Jesus is utterly dependable.

Now, listen to the words of praise to God which the priest says at Mass, at the end of the Eucharistic Prayer: 'Through him, and with him, and in him, O God, almighty Father, in the unity of the Holy Spirit, all glory and honour is yours, for ever and ever.' Once the priest recites those words, the congregation answers 'Amen'. This amen is called 'the great amen'. It is our 'yes', our acceptance of the terms and conditions of the Mass. Here, again, God only gives; our task is to accept. And so, when we present ourselves for Holy Communion, once again we say 'amen', before receiving the Body of Christ.

When we say 'amen' at the end of the Creed, we are saying our 'yes' to the gift of faith, to the wonderful, hope-filled, life-affirming, heart-warming truth that is ours as disciples. This little word commits us to being people of truth, to allowing the truth to shape our outlook and our dealings. Let us thank God for the gift of the faith that is our heritage and our hope, the faith that is summed up in the words and expressions of the Creed. Let us seek to love this faith, and to live a life that says 'I believe'. May it be so. Amen.

Conclusion

And After the 'Amen'?: Living the Creed

The Creed is incomplete. It does not mention prayer. It does not mention commandments or ethics. Aside from a solitary reference to Baptism, it does not mention the sacraments. Yet these things are essential to the living out of the faith. There are several reasons for these omissions. At the most practical level, the Creed was intended, from the beginning, for recitation during the liturgy. It had to be concise; it could not possibly cover everything. The Creed is not a catechism but a summary of the basics of Christian belief.

At a more fundamental level, the fact that the Creed does not deal with the living out of the faith tells us that the Christian life in its entirety follows from what God has done. The Creed, as we have seen, is all about God and God's actions. Even the section that deals with the Church does not refer to a single human initiative: the Church is God's work. It is striking to note that the only reference to a purely human action in the entire Creed is the reference to the crucifixion. Yes, the verb 'to believe' features four times, but it focuses entirely on God's nature and God's deeds.

The Creed, to repeat, is about what God has done. This simple fact has a profound consequence: the living out of the faith is only ever a response to what God has done. As the New Testament puts it, 'God loved us first' (1 Jn 4:19). Our response is not *in* the Creed, for the simple reason that it is a response *to* the Creed.

'God loved us first.' These words spell out in a short sentence what is often communicated in a single word: grace. God's gift is grace and God's grace is gift. It is unearned. It is unmerited. It does not consider what we deserve. We do not have to earn grace. Indeed we cannot. The Christian life in its entirety is an assent to what God has done and a 'yes' to grace.

Does this downplay the importance of our devotion, or of our efforts to live a life of integrity? Absolutely not; indeed, quite the contrary! All our initiatives, efforts and struggles in discipleship are a response to love. All our failures are a turning away from love. This ups the ante considerably. If the Christian life were an attempt to activate God, to invite his interest or win his favour, we could regard it as a means to an end. Our love for God could be seen as an attempt to pursue benefits of various kinds – right up to the benefit of eternal life.

But there is more at stake than benefits: what is at issue is a response to love. God's love has already been poured out – poured out in Christ's blood on the cross; poured into our hearts through the Holy Spirit (cf. Rm 5:5); poured into the Church through Baptism and the forgiveness of sins. We are invited to respond; we are free not to respond. This is an awesome freedom. It is the freedom at the heart of discipleship.

The Christian faith, from its fundamental convictions to its lived-out practices, has often been summed up in the words 'creed', 'code' and 'cult'. Creed is what we believe; code is how we live; and cult (from the Latin word *cultus*, meaning worship) is how we pray. Christian faith is not the Creed alone: it is the Creed and the response to the Creed. It is the work of a loving God, Father, Son and Spirit, who gathers us into the Church. And it is our membership of the Church, the fellowship in which we are called to live a life of charity and prayer.

Can there be any better way to live than as a response to love? Can there be any better plan for a person's life? The Creed, which we have sought to understand in these reflections, describes God's gift. The Christian life, which is our response, is about unwrapping that gift. It is a life of gratitude. In this life, neither our understanding nor our response will ever be complete; there will always be room for improvement; we will always be able to affirm that the best is yet to come. As we continue on our pilgrimage, let us exclaim with St Paul:

O the depth of the riches and wisdom and knowledge of God!
How unsearchable are his judgements
and how inscrutable his ways!
For from him and through him and to him
are all things.
To him be the glory forever.
Amen. (Rm 11:33, 36)